SECRET HISTORY OF THE
WILD, WILD
WEST

SECRET HISTORY OF THE
WILD, WILD
WEST

Outlaws, Secret Societies, and the Hidden Agenda of the Elites

DANIEL J. DUKE

DESTINY

BOOKS

Destiny Books
Rochester, Vermont

Destiny Books
One Park Street
Rochester, Vermont 05767
www.DestinyBooks.com

Text stock is SFI certified

Destiny Books is a division of Inner Traditions International

Cataloging-in-Publication Data for this title is available from the Library of Congress

ISBN 978-1-64411-229-8 (print)
ISBN 978-1-64411-230-4 (ebook)

Printed and bound in the United States by Lake Book Manufacturing, Inc. The text stock is SFI certified. The Sustainable Forestry Initiative® program promotes sustainable forest management.

10 9 8 7 6 5 4 3 2 1

Text design by Debbie Glogover and layout by Virginia Scott Bowman
This book was typeset in Garamond Premier Pro with Gill Sans and Empera used as display typfaces

To send correspondence to the author of this book, mail a first-class letter to the author c/o Inner Traditions • Bear & Company, One Park Street, Rochester, VT 05767, and we will forward the communication, or contact the author directly at **jessewjames.wordpress.com**.

For my late mother, mentor,
and favorite author, Betty Dorsett Duke.

I would like to express my most profound gratitude to my mother, Betty Dorsett Duke. Many thanks to my father, Joe Duke, for the help and tremendous support provided. And thank you to Teresa F. Duke, my sister. I am also grateful to have such a great literary agent, Fiona Spencer Thomas. A big thank you to my publisher and the team at Inner Traditions • Bear & Company. To Matt, thank you for all the help. I want to thank my friend, author and editor Philippa (Lee) Faulks for her support and for pointing me in the right direction.

CONTENTS

AN INTRODUCTION

In my first book, *Jesse James and the Lost Templar Treasure,* I wrote of the treasures associated with the Old West outlaw Jesse James. In the second book, *The Mysterious Life and Faked Death of Jesse James,* which I coauthored with my sister Teresa F. Duke, we unveiled the true history of Jesse James and showed that Jesse James is our great-great-grandfather. Those two books expose the history of the treasures associated with Jesse James and the truth about the events and investigations surrounding his alleged assassination.

This book will show you, dear reader, how Jesse James, the infamous outlaw, had connections with not only several well-known Old West outlaws, such as Billy the Kid, Jesse Evans, and Johnny Ringo, among others, but that he also had connections and was related—by blood or marriage—to people who, once you realize who they are, will very likely shock you.

But there is even more to the story of Jesse James's connections. He is also related, again by blood or marriage, to some of the best-known—and a few notorious—families of the American West. Families whose names carried a lot of weight in politics, religion, and even a secret society. Some of these families were even instrumental in the formation and leadership of a well-known and popular branch of church in the Bible belt, the Baptist church. The connections between Jesse James and the aforementioned (or hinted at) people and organizations, as well as many of the other Old West outlaws, show that they were much more than just wild cowboys who rode around randomly robbing and shooting people. They were actually organized, and part of something much larger: an organization that seems to have grown, prospered, and affected our national history from the small, rural streets of early America to the highest levels of our nation's government up to, at least, the very near present day. And just like any organization, they had their rivals. I invite you to read on to find out how this secret network with powerful and prestigious connections operated in America's Wild West and beyond. I suspect that you may, after reading this book, view history a bit differently, as it connects long-hidden puzzle pieces to those mysterious aspects of history over which many have pondered the nagging suspicion at their connections.

Jesse James

The Traditional Story

Jesse James is the man who represents every man who ever felt the boot of the Man on his neck.

LAURA JAMES, *THE LOVE PIRATE
AND THE BANDIT'S SON*

Over the years, Jesse James has been many things to many people. Jesse James was an outlaw to most, a hero to others; he was a rebel, a killer, a man done wrong by the powers that be, and to some, a terrorist. For better or worse, he has captured the minds of the public around the world. I am the first to admit that Jesse James was no angel, but he was no devil either, unless he had to be. How is it that a man who had been branded an outlaw could have had such a great impact on the minds of people around the globe for well over a century? Perhaps because of the perfect combination of fact and myth that surrounded him, both while he was living and long after his death.

A large part of the public's fascination no doubt has to do with people wanting the whole story—the truth, the whole truth, and nothing but the truth. Until they get answers, they won't be satisfied, and

Fig. 1.1. Photo of Jesse Woodson James, circa 1864.

neither will we. But the only truth readily available when talking about Jesse James is that the real truth is hard to come by.

The journey to prove that Jesse James is our ancestor has been an exciting one, to say the least. My siblings and I believe that Jesse James is our great-great-grandfather, a fact that our late mother set out to prove prior to her passing. Before digging into the mystery that surrounds Jesse and his network throughout the Wild West, here's the brief, traditionally accepted life of Jesse James.

EARLY YEARS

Jesse Woodson James is said to have been born on September 5, 1847, to Zerelda Elizabeth Cole and Robert Sallee James, an ordained Baptist minister and founder of William Jewell College in Liberty, Missouri. Jesse was the third of four children born to the couple. His older siblings were Alexander Franklin "Frank" James, the firstborn, and Robert R. James, who died as an infant. Susan Lavenia James was the couple's fourth child.

Apparently, shortly after Susan's birth, the elder Robert James felt the need to preach to gold miners in California. He left his wife and children in Missouri and, shortly after arriving in California in 1850, he is said to have contracted a disease (stories vary as to exactly what he caught), died, and was buried in an unmarked grave.

In 1852, after Robert's death, Zerelda married a wealthy farmer named Benjamin Simms. Mr. Simms is said to have been a cruel man who didn't like young Frank or Jesse. He died in a horse accident at the start of 1854. No children were born from the short marriage of Benjamin Simms and Zerelda.

Zerelda married, for a third and final time, in 1855, to Dr. Reuben Samuel. Dr. Samuel is said to have been a kind-hearted man and a loving father to Zerelda's children, Frank, Jesse, and Susan. Zerelda and Dr. Samuel had four children as well: Sarah Louisa Samuel, John Thomas Samuel, Fanny Quantrill Samuel, and Archie Peyton Samuel.

THE CIVIL WAR YEARS

Well before the official beginning of the American Civil War, tensions had been building along the Kansas and Missouri border between pro-slavery and antislavery factions. Militias formed on both sides of the border, and skirmishes soon followed. Frank James joined the Confederacy and is said to have fallen ill, which led him to return home to recuperate. During that time, Frank joined a pro-Confederate militia, Quantrill's Partisan Rangers, near his family home. A Union militia, looking for Frank, raided the James-Samuel farm. Zerelda related the story to a reporter many years later:

> I remember well that morning the soldiers came down across the field. It was planted in flax then. A whole company of them came

down through there and trooped into this yard, and over into the field where Jesse and Dr. Samuels* were planting corn. They demanded the doctor tell them where the bushwhackers were hiding. You see Frank was four years older than Jesse and had been with Quantrill over a year. . . . Dr. Samuels, my husband told them he did not know where the bushwhackers were. Then they tied his hands together and drove him to a tree over in the pasture and hanged him three times by the neck. They left him hanging until he was nearly dead and then lowered him down and asked where Frank James was. They left him at last, nearly dead, under the tree. The doctor has not been in his right mind since that very day and he was a smart man.

But the cowardly hounds did not stop at hanging the doctor. They caught my little Jesse, he was only fourteen years old then and sickly, and they ran him up and down the corn rows, prodding him with their bayonets and threatening to kill him if he didn't tell them where his brother Frank was.

But there wasn't a drop of coward's blood in the veins of my Jesse. How many boys do you know think [*sic*] would have braved that gang of armed cowards as he did that day? They prodded him with their sharp bayonets till the blood ran and then they beat his poor back till for weeks afterward he could scarcely wear a shirt. It was then that the hatred of Federal soldiers was put into his heart and it never left him.

A day or two after that Jesse told me he was going to join Quantrill and take a hand in this fight. Jesse was small for his age and very sickly and thin, and I was afraid to have him go off in the bush with Quantrill. I told him he was too young and small for that kind of rough work, and besides he had no money.

---

*Officially, Samuel, without an *s,* was the last name of the doctor who married Zerelda. Many historians and journalists have mistakenly added an *s* to the last name over the years.

He told me strength and money will both come with time. I fitted him out with clothes, gave him some money, and one of our horses and he rode away to join Quantrill. I didn't hear a word from him till about three months after that when a tall young man rode up and hitched his horse at the gate and knocked at the door. I didn't know him till he laughed and then I saw it was my Jesse, and I guess it wasn't a second till I had him in my arms. The wild life in the bush had agreed with him and he was rosy cheeked and stout. That was the beginning of my boy's roving and from that time till this, more than thirty years, I've never had a full night's rest since.[1]

In short, Jesse followed his older brother, Frank, in joining Quantrill's guerrillas in 1864. While they rode with the guerrillas, Union officials forced their family to leave not only their farm but also the county they lived in. Dr. Samuel, Zerelda, and their children temporarily relocated to Nebraska during that time.

During the war, it is generally believed that Jesse suffered a bullet through his right lung but returned to fighting after healing. It is also said that at the end of the war, while trying to surrender, he was shot once again through the right lung. We have no reason to doubt this. When trying to obtain a death certificate or coroner's report for Jesse (who, at the time of his death, was going by the name James L. Courtney), we were told that his death records had been destroyed approximately one year before we inquired about them.

THE OUTLAW YEARS

While the war was officially over, former guerrillas, like Jesse and Frank James, weren't granted amnesty. They were hunted, and because of that, the war couldn't end for them. They probably took the attitude that if they were to be labeled outlaws, they might as well be outlaws. Not too long afterward, the James-Younger Gang came into being.

The Liberty bank robbery on February 13, 1866, may be the first robbery accredited to the James-Younger Gang, and it is considered to be the first successful peacetime daylight bank robbery in the United States. At two o'clock in the afternoon, twelve men wearing faded soldier-blue overcoats rode into Liberty from various directions, congregating in front of the Clay County Savings Association Bank. No great interest was taken in these men, since this was shortly after the end of the Civil War, and Liberty had been occupied a number of times by groups of men.

Two men entered the bank and found Greenup Bird, head cashier, and his son and assistant, William, inside. One of the robbers requested a bill to be changed (this would become the modus operandi of the James-Younger Gang). William Bird approached the counter, and as he did, both robbers drew their guns, demanding that the clerks quickly deposit the money into an empty feed sack. Once the money, bonds, and tax stamps were deposited, both Birds were placed in a cage (the vault).

The robbers departed the bank, and as they were mounting their horses, a commotion took place. One man appeared to have some difficulty with his horse. Across the street, at the Green Hotel, two boys were watching. There are several local and family stories regarding what happened in the next few minutes. In any event, a shooting killed George "Jolly" Wymore, one of the two boys observing the ruckus. Although Jesse James has been blamed for it, most accounts claim he did not shoot Jolly Wymore.

The Wymore family has passed down the story that within a few weeks they received a letter apologizing for the death of the boy. The letter also stated that no one was supposed to be harmed, and it was signed "Jesse James." (We have requested to see this letter but to no avail.) The Wymore family still owns this building, and named it the Jesse James Bank Museum. When we asked if they ever displayed the letter, the tour guide explained that it was too traumatic for the owner to display.

There are two strongly opposing views about whether Jesse James was at the scene of the robbery. By one view, this was shortly after the Civil War, and Jesse had recently received a serious chest wound, collapsing one of his lungs and leaving him too ill to be present. Others note the local stories of a man who appeared to be ill and reportedly had trouble staying mounted. They believe this to be Jesse. The contention is that if he planned this robbery in such detail, he would not have missed the event. During the getaway, several people later admitted that they recognized many of the boys.

Reportedly there is little doubt that Jesse James planned the robbery because it was styled after many of the robberies the men participated in during the Civil War. During the Civil War much of what soldiers did was considered acts of war and not crimes. Some claim they were barbaric while others claim the same about the other side. Perhaps the concept "to the victor goes the spoils" applies as history often sides with the victor. No one was ever convicted of the Liberty robbery, which caused the bank to close because of insufficient funds. The bank sold all its assets, called in all loans, and paid the depositors sixty cents on the dollar.

Many other robberies that took place between 1867 and 1881, all across the midwestern and southern United States, were alleged to be the handiwork of the James-Younger Gang. The robbery at the First National Bank in Northfield, Minnesota, September 7, 1876, is credited as breaking up the James-Younger Gang and being their last robbery. It may be true that the James-Younger Gang was impacted by the failed Northfield robbery, but we don't believe the failure resulted in the end of the gang. Jesse and Frank had a pool of irregular members to choose from, and it is our opinion that the gang didn't come to an end until the alleged assassination of Jesse James, if in name only, in 1882. In Northfield, the town's citizens ambushed the riders from the hardware store and the second floor of the hotel, thwarting the robbery attempt. Most sources claim that Frank James was responsible for the death of Joseph L. Heywood, the bank cashier who refused to open the safe. While at least one source claims it was Jesse who killed the cashier, we don't believe that Jesse was at the robbery and that his first cousin, Wood Hite, who bore a strong resemblance to Jesse, was mistaken for him. Other persons in the bank included A. E. Bunker, cashier (shot in the shoulder), and Frank J. Wilcox, assistant bookkeeper. Gang members Clell Miller and Bill Chadwell were reportedly killed in the streets. During the escape, all three Younger brothers, Cole, Jim, and Bob, were captured and imprisoned, and Charley Pitts a.k.a. Sam Wells was killed. Frank James and his first cousin Wood Hite escaped, with Frank making his way to Texas. Frank had the bullet he received in Northfield surgically removed in Waco, Texas.[2] This statement is verified by a sheriff's notes on an old wanted poster purchased at the Jesse James Farm and Museum in Kearney, Missouri, which also said that the Youngers were tried and served twenty-five years in Minnesota's Stillwater Prison, and that Frank and Jesse reportedly stayed in Texas until they returned to their old haunts in Clay County, Missouri.[3]

In spite of the sheer number of robberies Jesse James is alleged to have organized or participated in, he was never caught. He had many aliases and identities, which greatly assisted him in eluding capture for sixteen years. For years, he was hunted by many to no avail, including by the Pinkerton National Detective Agency, and frustrations were growing.

The Pinkerton Agency, founded by Scotsman Allan Pinkerton in 1850, played an important role in U.S. history, foiling an attempted assassination of the newly elected president, Abraham Lincoln, in 1861 and serving as intelligence agents for the federal government during the Civil War. The Pinkertons also specialized in protecting railroad shipments for several Midwestern companies. When the first recorded train robbery took place in 1866, they became famous for their pursuit of train robbers—including the James-Younger Gang, which they were under contract from both the railroads and the banks to apprehend.

The Pinkertons were known for playing things rough. On January 26, 1875, Jesse James's eight-year-old half brother, Archie Peyton Samuel, was killed by a bomb that was thrown into their home by Pinkerton detectives. Jesse's mother lost the lower portion of an arm, and one of his stepfather's hands was maimed.

With a $10,000 reward on his head, Jesse is said to have moved his family to St. Joseph, Missouri, in November 1881.[4] On Christmas Eve, Jesse, reportedly using the alias of Thomas Howard, along with Zee Mimms* and their two reported children, Tim and Mary Howard, moved into a small house at 1318 Lafayette Street, sitting atop a high hill overlooking St. Joseph.†

Several months later, on April 3, 1882, Bob Ford reportedly shot Jesse James dead while Jesse was dusting a picture. On that very day, a train was robbed in Texas, and newspapers all over all the country attributed it to Jesse.[5]

This was just the beginning of the mystery surrounding Jesse's death, causing many to feel bewildered to this day. The event has stirred many emotions in people from all walks of life, including Oscar Wilde, who said, "Americans are certainly great hero-worshippers, and always take heroes from the criminal classes." Many opinions on Jesse sprang forth after his alleged death—some good and some bad. Jesse has been regarded as a Robin Hood of that era; some even likened him to King Arthur.

---

*Some claim that Jesse fell in love with his first cousin, Zerelda "Zee" Mimms, who may have helped him recover from the wound he received near the end of the war. Note that the surname *Mimms* is oftentimes spelled with either one or two letter *m*s. When quoting a source I have spelled it the way the source spells it; if not quoted I have spelled it *Mimms*.

†The problem with this theory is that we believe Jesse was already living in Texas by this time. We also don't believe Jesse James married Zee Mimms. We believe Zee actually married another of Jesse's first cousins, Wood Hite. This is probable for several reasons. First, though they may have just lived together, their families being upstanding, traditional Baptists before the Civil War points to a probable marriage. However, when our mother asked the Missouri State Archives for records of marriage for Jesse and Zee, there were none to be had, nor were there any for Wood and Zee, nor were there any other records for any aliases for Jesse James, his first cousin Wood Hite, or for Zee Mimms as being married to anyone. One must remember that Wood Hite was also a wanted man, making it possible that an alias may have been used on marriage documents.

After Jesse's reported assassination, the authorities, suspecting that the deceased was not Jesse, paid round-trip transportation expenses from Texas to St. Joseph, Missouri, for Harrison Trow and five other gunmen who had once worked with him. They hoped these men would either identify the body as Jesse's or confirm their suspicions that it was not his body. Trow glanced momentarily at the corpse and remarked tonelessly as he walked away, "That's Jesse." But another gunman who rode with Jesse said it wasn't: "In 1882, after Jesse's alleged death, former James Gang member George Shepard said he had been down town and had seen the picture posted in the Times window purporting to be a likeness of Jesse James. He had no hesitation in declaring that if that was a true picture of the man killed in St. Joseph, it wasn't Jesse James at all."[6]

A coroner's inquest was held to determine if the man Bob Ford shot was really Jesse James. Accurate physical descriptions of the famous outlaw were non-existent except to a chosen few. In his book *Goodbye Jesse James*, which included reprints of six news stories covering the alleged assassination of Jesse James, editor Jack Wymore wrote, "It is safe to say there is no picture of Jesse James in existence that will convey a correct impression of his appearance in life."[7]

There are conflicting reports of his physical appearance, including his scars, making it hard to know if anyone identifying his body was accurate. Traditionalists, for example, describe Jesse James as being between five feet nine to five feet eleven, with a small frame, blue eyes, a missing fingertip, and light, sandy-colored hair. But many agree there is no definitive proof that Jesse James was missing a fingertip, and there is evidence that those who knew him best, including his own mother, described him as being tall.

- His mother described him as "tall and stout."[8]
- John T. Samuel, Jesse's half-brother, testified at Frank James's trial that "Jesse was a large man."[9]
- John Newman Edwards, who had been General J. O. Shelby's

adjutant during the Civil War and afterward became the editor of the *Kansas City Times*, met Jesse during the war. A good friend, he described him as "tall and finely molded capable of great effort and endurance."[10]

- Jesse James described himself as tall. After a train robbery at Gads Hill, Missouri on January 31, 1874, he handed the conductor a press release that partially described the gang: "The robbers were all large men, none under six feet tall."

The coroner's ruling that Bob Ford did shoot Jesse James did not stop the general public from doubting it. An article appearing in the *St. Joseph Daily Gazette* from St. Joseph, Missouri, on April 12, 1882, attempted to explain why the corpse's hair was darker than Jesse James's was known to be:

One of the most successful means of concealing identity used by the famous freebooter Jesse James was accidentally discovered yesterday. A Gazette reporter learned the facts from headquarters and can vouch for their authenticity.

It has been handed down through all the fables regarding Jesse that he was of a light complexion, that his beard and hair were rather light and of a reddish hue. This statement has been corroborated by parties claiming to know him, and with his bluish gray eyes, a lighter color of hair and beard might have been expected than existed at the time of death. Yesterday a gentleman was sitting in the room where Mrs. James was at work packing a valise preparatory to departure. As she bent over her work, a small vial dropped to the floor and broke, whereupon a dark brown liquid began to run over the carpet. The gentleman picked it up, and naturally enough asked what the substance might be. Mrs. James seemed embarrassed, and at that did not know what to say. She finally, however, said that it was a kind of dye used by her husband for coloring his hair and beard. Mrs. James had endeavored to conceal this ruse of her husband to prevent identification and requested that nothing be said about the matter. This little fact will explain away the doubts of many skeptics regarding the identity of the murdered man.[11]

A funeral was held, but our family strongly believes it wasn't Jesse in the casket.* Whether or not he died and was buried as history says, the myths surrounding him have lived on to the present day.

THE ALIAS

So what if it wasn't Jesse in the casket? What events had previously transpired that would have allowed him to fake his own death? After the failed bank robbery in Northfield, Minnesota in 1876 in which the original gang was virtually wiped out, with virtually only Jesse and Frank remaining, Frank James rode a train from Minnesota all the way south to Waco, Texas, and was said to have visited an unknown doctor in Waco to take care of the bullet wounds he had suffered in Northfield. Frank was also said to have been met by Jesse in Waco, and, after Frank was ready to travel, they went to Jesse's ranch in Blevins, Texas, approximately twenty-two miles south of Waco. We don't believe Jesse was at the Northfield robbery but that it was his first cousin Wood Hite who was oftentimes mistaken for Jesse. Jesse was at his home in Blevins at the time.

It is said that outlaws often chose aliases from names they were familiar with. Jesse, our great-great-grandfather, wrote the following rhyme in his diary: "When stemm [sic] and tryst James L. Courtney is my heist." Stemm, or stem, refers here to a line of descendants from

---

*We believe the body thought to be Jesse James was actually Jesse's cousin Wood Hite. Others believe the real Thomas Howard, whose name Jesse had been using as an alias at that time, may have been passed off for Jesse. Still others claimed a man by the name of Charley Bigelow was the true identity of the body. For more on this topic, see the book I cowrote with my sister, Teresa F. Duke, *The Mysterious Life and Faked Death of Jesse James.*

a particular ancestor; a tryst is a place of a prearranged meeting (a variant pronunciation is with a long vowel, which would rhyme with heist); and heist is, of course, a robbery. I believe my great-great-grandfather stole the name of his relative James L. Courtney at a secret prearranged meeting. There are many reasons to believe the James family was linked with the Courtneys.

Historical reports state that three families of Courtneys lived near the James farm in Clay County, Missouri.

Reverend Robert James, father of Frank and Jesse, baptized and married Courtneys.[12]

The probate papers of Reverend Robert James show that A. C. Courtney tutored Frank James and Jesse James. The same papers show that Joseph Courtney and his wife joined New Hope Baptist Church under Rev. James and said, "There is no better man than Robert James."

Frank James borrowed a plow from his Courtney neighbors.[13]

Jesse James's two half sisters had Courtney connections. Sarah Louisa Samuel married William A. Nicholson, whose paternal grandmother was Lucinda Courtney. Fannie Quantrill Samuel married Joe Hall, whose mother was Rebecca Ann Courtney.[14]

Jesse R. Cole, Frank and Jesse James's maternal uncle, married Louisa E. Maret, and they had a daughter named Bettie. Bettie Cole married James Courtney in Clay County, Missouri. After James died, she married Elias Albright.[15] Louisa's brother, John M. Maret, married Annie Jane Lucinda Courtney.[16]

Thomas Edward "Bud" Pence and Alexander Doniphan "Donnie" Pence of Clay County Missouri rode with the James-Younger Gang.[17] Their sister, America Lorena Pence, married James Clinton Courtney in Clay County.[18]

A neighboring Courtney complimented Zerelda James Samuel's embroidery work, saying, "Our family said that Jesse James' mother could do beautiful embroidery despite the loss of part of her arm, lost in the tragedy [Pinkerton bombing] at the time Jesse's little brother

[Archie Samuel] was killed, 26 Jan. 1875. I was told she would place the fabric over the stub to do her stitches."[19]

W. J. Courtney was a sheriff and attorney of Clay County during Frank and Jesse's outlaw years. He was also in the same home guard unit as Frank James, along with many other Courtneys.[20] During the Civil War, he was with General Joseph O. Shelby's brigade[21] (Quantrill and his men often aligned themselves with Shelby's brigade). W. J. Courtney owned and operated the Arthur House in Liberty, Missouri, where Pinkerton detective John W. Whicher was served his last meal on Earth before being found dead the next morning on the road to the James farm.[22] The James boys were accused of his murder.

A document referred to as a "true bill"* regarding the Pinkerton bombing at the James-Samuel farm shows that W. J. Courtney was one of the witnesses.[23]

Census records from 1860 show that the real James L. Courtney lived in Johnson County, Missouri, with his parents, Stephen and Dinah Courtney.[24] In January 1986, the *Pioneer Times* stated, "They [The Courtneys] were related to the Courtneys and the James of Clay County, Missouri."[25] Both the Clay County and Johnson County Courtney families are related to the James-Samuel family.†

On July 6, 1863, A. C. Courtney, along with two other neighbors,

---

*A true bill is the written and signed decision of a grand jury that it has heard sufficient evidence from the prosecution to believe that a crime has been committed and the accused should stand trial.

†The founding of Jesse James's family goes as follows: Sarah Mason married Andrew Barbee. When he died, she married Thomas James in the 1670s, and these are our earliest founding ancestors that we know of on the James side (information from the Stafford Will and Parish records; Thomas Barbee's will dated November 8, 1748; State Archives; Overwharton Parish Records by GeoSanford Harrison King; Fauquier County Marriages for Barbee; Carol Holmes also provided some of this information in a now-extinct aol forum; the website "Barbee Crossroads" verifies Sarah Elizabeth Mason first married Andrew Barbee and then, after Barbee's death, Thomas James). The Courtney family came out of the line of Andrew Barbee and the James family came out of the Thomas James line.

Mr. Larkin and Alvah Maret, signed an affidavit and gave it to the provost marshal in Liberty, Missouri, in an effort to obtain Dr. Samuel's release from military prison.

There are at least ten tombstones bearing the Courtney name in Kearney's Mount Olivet Cemetery. One tombstone bears the name of James Courtney.

In a notarized affidavit by Michelle Archie from June 1, 1999, Howard Smith Farmer said that he heard his grandmother Vesta Farmer, born in 1879, tell her brother, John Mile, that Jesse James was buried in Blevins Cemetery under the name of James L. Courtney.

The 1880 census records for Susan James Parmer, Jesse James's sister, show that she lived with her husband, Allen H. Parmer, son Robert A., and daughters Clora S. and Zelma in Henrietta, Clay County, Texas. At another of several locations where the Parmers lived in Texas, a Texas historical marker marks the Parmer house as a Jesse James hideout.* Jack Loftin, a historian from Archer County, Texas, wrote in his book *Trails through Archer*:

> A daughter of Jesse's niece, Allen Palmer's† granddaughter, has told an Archer City Historical Commission that in her mother's trunk are many letters, some of which will prove that Jesse wrote to his sister, her grandmother, dated and postmarked Henrietta, Texas 1884. These letters the mother had planned to burn, but they are not lost, have been promised to the county commission.[26]

During our research, we located many connections between the James family and the Courtneys that led us to believe that Jesse James assumed the Courtney surname well before he decided to fake his

---

*The house is located at Courthouse Lawn, Highway 79, Center Street, Archer City, Texas. The Archer City marker was erected in 1972.

†Census takers often mix up the spelling of names. The source used *Palmer* but the surname should have been *Parmer*.

death in 1882. Each piece of evidence indicates that Jesse James did not die on April 3, 1882. Instead, by this time he had officially killed his name, assumed the name of James L. Courtney, and had hightailed it to Blevins, Texas, where he lived to be almost a century old. Along the way, and once settled in Texas, he would rub elbows with some of the most influential outlaws and men of politics of his time.

BILLY THE KID
THE TRADITIONAL STORY

Another Old West character who, much like Jesse James, seems to have risen above the stigma of outlaw and reached the lofty status of Old West hero to many is Billy the Kid.* Both Jesse and Billy were perceived by many in their day and afterward as having been given a raw deal. While they were definitely not angelic, they managed to appeal in a favorable light to the masses.

The historically accepted version of Billy's demise, including how he allegedly died at the hands of a trusted ally, shares a strikingly similar arc to Jesse's story. It's the kind of story that evokes great animosity toward the alleged perpetrator of such a heinous deed—killing your fellow outlaw, friend, and partner in crime—especially when that assassination was committed in the same backstabbing, cowardly manner as that which was supposedly done to Jesse James.

Billy the Kid is said to have been born in either September or November of 1859, in New York City, to Catherine Devine and

---

*The character I am speaking of is Henry McCarty a.k.a. William H. Bonney a.k.a. Billy the Kid. So as to prevent any confusion for the reader, I will refer to him by his most well-known moniker, Billy the Kid, or simply Billy, throughout the remainder of this book.

Fig. 2.1. Photo of Billy the Kid.

Patrick McCarty. Patrick McCarty is said to have died while Billy and his younger brother, Joseph, were children. Shortly after Patrick's death, Billy's mother, Catherine, moved west, stopping in Indianapolis, Indiana, where she met Billy and Joseph's future stepfather, William Henry Harrison Antrim. In 1870 Antrim and the McCarty family were in Wichita, Kansas, and then moved to Santa Fe, New Mexico, where Mr. Antrim and Catherine McCarty were married in 1873. The following year, 1874, Billy's mother is said to have died from tuberculosis in September. Shortly after her death, Patrick Antrim abandoned Billy and Joseph, leaving them to fend for themselves. Billy was fifteen years old.

From there, Billy began his trek into outlaw history, starting with small thefts and working his way up to stealing horses in various locations throughout the American Southwest. In 1877, when he was about seventeen years old, Billy killed his first man, a blacksmith who had bullied him. It was said that Billy had no choice as the two fought for control of Billy's revolver and Billy got the upper hand. Billy fled the scene and was apprehended several days later, placed in jail, and soon afterward made his first jail break. After escaping jail, he had his horse confiscated by Apache Indians and eventually made his way across the desert to the home of a friend, where he was nursed back to health. That friend was John Jones, a member of a gang known as the Seven Rivers Warriors. Billy healed and left the area for a time, making his way to Lincoln County, New Mexico, rustling cattle from famed cattle baron John Chisholm.

Billy then went to work for cattle rancher John Henry Tunstall, who had been in an ongoing feud with a faction of powerful men who had created an "alliance formed by Irish-American businessmen Lawrence Murphy, James Dolan, and John Riley. The three men had wielded an economic and political hold over Lincoln County since the early 1870s, due in part to their ownership of a beef contract with nearby Fort Stanton and a well-patronized dry goods store in the town of Lincoln."[1] In February of 1878 the feuding had reached a new low when John Henry Tunstall was stopped by a group of men hired by the Murphy-Dolan faction, disarmed, and shot in the back of the head. The murder of Tunstall added fuel to an already hot fire and led to what became known as the Lincoln County War.

The Lincoln County War in New Mexico in turn led to a chaotic atmosphere, with people being deputized on both sides. Even the U.S. military had a small role to play. It was this "war" that brought Billy the Kid from being known as a local bandit to a famous—or rather, infamous—outlaw. Billy rode with the Regulators, a group that at the time amounted to roughly sixty men. Billy and other members of the Regulators holed up in lawyer Alexander McSween's home.

McSween was killed in the battle, and three surviving members of the battle escaped, one of those being Billy.

On the run, hiding out and being chased while additional murders were being blamed on Billy and his gang, Billy reached out to the territorial governor of New Mexico, Lew Wallace. "Wallace agreed to meet with him in Lincoln. Wallace, who wanted to break up what he considered a corrupt faction, promised the Kid that if he would testify against Dolan, he would not be prosecuted for the killing of Sheriff Brady. The Kid agreed, and on April 14 he provided testimony that resulted in Evans and Dolan's being indicted for [attorney Huston] Chapman's murder."[2] There was a problem however, as the district attorney at the time was a Dolan supporter. "After letting Dolan and Evans go, he ordered the Kid confined to jail. Though Billy the Kid wrote letters to Governor Wallace reminding him of his promise of amnesty, the Kid remained a prisoner. At first opportunity, he escaped."[3]

On the night of July 14, 1881, Billy the Kid was said to have been near Fort Sumner, New Mexico, at the ranch of a man by the name of Pete Maxwell. Pat Garrett, Billy's old friend, was now a sheriff and snuck onto the ranch with two deputies, John Poe and Tom McKinney. Pat was said to have taken position with Pete Maxwell inside Pete's quarters while the two deputies waited outside. Billy was said to have entered the room unexpectedly and, peering into the dark, uttered in Spanish, *"Quien es?"* ("Who is it?") "Sudden movement near the rear wall catches his attention, and he peers into the darkness. Seeing Maxwell rise to a seated position on the bed, he is about to speak again when a gunshot explodes, then another. Knocked backward from the impact of a bullet, the young man drops his knife and collapses to the floor near the open doorway, blood oozing from a wound in his chest. From behind a bed, a shaken Pat Garrett rises to his full height and takes one cautious step toward the prone, somewhat frail-looking body on Maxwell's floor. Then, he turns and dashes out the doorway to find Poe and McKinney waiting."[4] Pat announced to his deputies that it was the Kid. But was it?

That is how Billy is said to have met his fate—according to traditionally accepted history, that is. There are, however, alternate versions, and it is the opinion of a growing number of researchers that Billy the Kid, like Jesse James, faked his death.

Billy was said to have died in 1881, and Jesse was said to have died in 1882. Now normally I wouldn't have thought twice about two men dying so close together—roughly eight and a half months apart—but after all of the research my family and I have done over the years, and the connections we have discovered that link Jesse James and Billy the Kid together in various ways, I can't help but wonder if the two men planned it that way.

As after the death of Jesse James, numerous men came forward over the years following Billy the Kid's death claiming to be Billy the Kid, and most of them were easily proven to be false. One claimant who wasn't so easily disproven is a man by the name of Oliver P. "Ollie" Roberts a.k.a. "Brushy Bill" Roberts of Hico, Texas, who claimed to be the infamous Billy the Kid. It just so happens that he is listed in my great-great-grandfather's diary.

In Cahoots

THE MEETING

It is very likely that Jesse James and Billy the Kid lived in the same area at the same time and, in fact, they most likely knew each other. A fascinating link tying Jesse and Billy together is an account of their meeting in Las Vegas, New Mexico, in 1879. In a book published in 1929 and titled *A Frontier Doctor,* Henry F. Hoyt, the author, describes a night in July 1879 when he saw his old friend Billy the Kid and met the outlaw Jesse James. It happened at a restaurant and hotel six miles outside of Las Vegas, New Mexico, owned by Scott Moore and his wife, Minnie Moore. The following is Henry F. Hoyt's description of the meeting:

> "I rode out one Sunday and found at a corner table the only vacant seat in the room. Glancing at the three guests already there, I was perfectly amazed to recognize the one on my left as Billy the Kid, urbane and smiling as ever. We shook hands, but neither mentioned a name.
>
> We were chatting away of old times in Texas as if we were a couple of cowboy friends, when the man on Bonney's* left made a

---

*Henry McCarty a.k.a. Billy the Kid was said by many to have used the alias William Harrison Bonney. The New World Encyclopedia states: "Henry McCarty (November 23, 1859–July 14, 1881) was better known as Billy the Kid, but also known by the aliases Henry Antrim and William Harrison Bonney."

comment on something he said. Whereupon Billy said, 'Hoyt, meet my friend Mr. Howard from Tennessee.'

The fourth man had nearly finished his meal when I sat down and soon retired. Mr. Howard had noticeable characteristics. He had piercing steely blue eyes with a peculiar blink, and the tip of a finger on his left hand was missing. I mentally classed him as a railroad man. He proved to be congenial, was a good talker, had evidently traveled quite a bit, and the meal passed pleasantly. After dinner we separated and Billy, taking me to his room, gave me, after pledging me to secrecy, one of the surprises of my life. Mr. Howard was no other than the bandit and train robber, Jesse James."[1]

The timeline of the previous quote by author Henry F. Hoyt fits with Jesse's timeline. Jesse was said to have been trying to rebuild his gang at the time after the gang's disastrous 1876 bank robbery attempt in Northfield, Minnesota, had failed.

Bill Markley, author of *Billy the Kid and Jesse James: Outlaws of the Legendary West*, adds some additional information about the man who Henry F. Hoyt mentions. He writes that "Jesse took a trip on the Atchison, Topeka and Santa Fe Railway, riding the rails to the end of the line, Las Vegas, New Mexico Territory. From July 26 to 29, he visited old Missouri friends Scott Moore and his wife, Minnie, who ran a hotel and bathhouse at hot springs six miles outside of town."[2]

Author Ted P. Yeatman writes in his book *Frank and Jesse James: The Story Behind the Legend* that "in the summer of 1879, Jesse very likely made a trip west of the Mississippi that took him as far as the railhead of the new Santa Fe line at Las Vegas in northern New Mexico Territory, either to relocate there and escape creditors as he attempted to 'go straight,' or to operate in the area with a new gang. He was at least sizing it up as he visited with an old friend from Missouri, Scott Moore, who with his wife ran a hotel and bathhouse at the hot springs about six miles from town. It was here that the rather remarkable meeting probably took place between two of the most legendary American

POOR MAN'S AUTO THAT SELLS FOR $100

Hardly larger than a toy, this automobile attracted a great deal of attention at the Paris auto show. It is two and one-half horse power and it plus a speed of over twenty miles an hour. The price is only $100.

He Dined With Jesse James
and Billy the Kid!

Jesse James

The Frontier Doctor

Billy the Kid

A Bill of Sale from Billy the Kid

ROADS GET PART OF MOTOR COST

Ten Per Cent of Motoring Bill Goes to Highways in Minnesota.

THE MOTOR QUIZ
(How Many Can You Answer?)

By ELMO SCOTT WATSON

AUTOMOBILE NOTES

Fig. 3.1. A March 25, 1930, issue of the *Lampasas Daily Leader* printed an article titled "He Dined With Jesse James and Billy the Kid!" Lampasas, Tex., Vol. 27, no. 16, ed. 1 Tuesday, March 25, 1930.

outlaws of all time."[3] Yeatman goes on to describe the meeting according to the account given by Henry Hoyt, which I provided on page 24.

While research has proven some of Yeatman's theories to be wrong, especially those regarding the alleged death of Jesse James, it was nice to see that even he realized that Jesse was trying to "go straight," as evidenced several months later in the same year, 1879, when Jesse first attempted to fake his own death with the help of his fellow gang member, George Shepherd.

Yeatman goes further in revealing that "at least one other man claimed to have met Jesse at the same time. Miguel Ortero, later to serve as the territorial governor of New Mexico from 1897 to 1906, was working for his father's commission house and bank in Las Vegas when Jesse visited there. He too frequented the hotel dining hall, having known Moore in Kansas when Moore was working as a freight conductor there. Ortero met Howard in the dining room the day before Hoyt met him there. Moore had tipped him off about the stranger's identity but had sworn him to secrecy. Ortero recalled Jesse as 'noticeably quiet and reserved' with 'piercing' blue eyes."[4]

TIPS FROM THE DIARY

Another bit of information illustrating a potential link between Billy the Kid and Jesse James was found in the diary of my great-great-grandfather, J. L. Courtney a.k.a. Jesse James, when he mentioned the name of John Hittson, a famous Texas cattle baron. John Hittson's paternal uncle married Eliza Jane James, a verified relative of Jesse and Frank James.[5] John Hittson was at one time a business partner of John Chisum, the famous New Mexico cattle baron whose cattle had, at one or several times, been rustled by Billy the Kid and his gang.

Also mentioned in Jesse's diary was a man he called Colonel Pickett in Decatur, Texas. Colonel Pickett was Colonel George Bible Pickett, who lived near Decatur in Wise County, Texas. During the American Civil War, Pickett was the head of the Confederate Army camp near

Decatur, Texas. Colonel Pickett had a son named Tom Pickett, who rode with Billy the Kid for a time. Tom's occupations ranged from Texas Ranger to outlaw and several occupations in between. Like many Texas Rangers in the Old West, the line between law and outlaw was thin and it is actually quite common to read of Rangers who rode both sides of that thin line from time to time.

Further evidence points to the fact that Billy the Kid did not die at the hand of Pat Garrett and that Billy the Kid was known by our great-great-grandfather, who mentioned him in his diary as Wm Roberts. This Wm Roberts could be Brushy Bill Roberts, who is mentioned in an article by Brian Haines.

> In 1949, a lawyer named William Morrison met an old gunslinger named Jesse Evans. Evans told Morrison of his days fighting in the Lincoln County War, as well as stories about the war's most notable figure, Billy the Kid. Evans also claimed Billy the Kid, who was shot and killed by Pat Garrett, was not dead and was living under the alias of Brushy Bill Roberts.
>
> Morrison met with Roberts and confronted him. Though Roberts initially denied the claim, he later confessed that he was Billy the Kid. He asked Morrison to help grant him a pardon for his crimes. Morrison agreed and the two went before a judge.[6]

It is probable that Billy the Kid faked his death and lived under the alias of Brushy Bill Roberts near Hico, Texas, which is located approximately sixty miles northwest of Waco and seventy-two miles northwest of Blevins, and which is where our great-great-grandfather took up residence. Jesse's diary says as much—around July 23, 1872, Jesse recorded a list of names and residencies and there, in the midst of this list, is the name Wm Roberts (a.k.a. Wm for William a.k.a. Brushy Bill a.k.a. Billy the Kid). The evidence points to the fact that both men lived in the same region, at the same time, and likely even associated with one another.

Both men relocating within a day's ride of one another in Texas gives a little fuel for thought. Did they plan this? Was the meeting they had in Las Vegas, New Mexico, about rebuilding a gang, or was it about getting out while the getting was good?

The many similarities between the stories of Jesse James and Billy the Kid suggest that the two may have operated more closely than anyone realized. Take, for example, the details of their alleged deaths. Just as with Jesse's alleged assassination, the alleged assassination of Billy the Kid was also surrounded with mystery and many uncertainties. And the historically accepted demises of both men are almost mirror images of one another. But when it gets down to the fine details, the traditional stories of the assassinations of both men have nothing but emotion and hearsay backing them up. In light of Jesse and Billy's meeting in Las Vegas, New Mexico, less than a year before Billy's alleged death followed by Jesse's alleged death roughly eight months later, could it really be a coincidence that both men were killed by men they trusted? Combined with evidence my family has that they not only lived near each other but most likely knew each other, these likenesses seem like more than coincidence and suggest the two may have worked together.

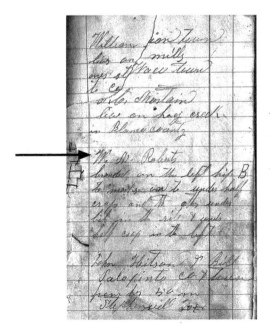

The page from Jesse's diary showing the name Wm. Roberts, thought to be Billy the Kid, as well as John and Bill Hitson, Texas cattlemen.

Outlaws with a Higher Purpose

Both Jesse and Billy faked their deaths and relocated to Texas, but did they change? Did they quit their outlaw ways and live upstanding lives or did they just change tactics? I believe they changed their tactics, in a sense, and toned down their actions. But that brings to mind another set of questions: Were they on a mission? What was their goal? Based on treasures Jesse was known to have buried, he had more than enough wealth to live comfortably for the rest of his long life and set his children up so that they could live comfortably. I hinted in my first book, *Jesse James and the Lost Templar Treasure,* at possible reasons for the treasures and what they could have been used for. In this chapter I will expand on that as well as discuss how getting away with faking their deaths in addition to the activities that Jesse James, Billy the Kid, and a few other outlaws were involved in, would have required some form of protection.

One source of protection was the Freemasons. Jesse James, under his alias of James Lafayette Courtney, "belonged to the Carolina Lodge in the Carolina Community, No. 330, District 17 from 1876–1884 when he demitted to join the Mooreville Lodge, number 639, probably because it was closer to his home in Blevins [Texas]."[1]

So we know that Jesse was James L. Courtney and under that alias he was a Freemason. Was he a Freemason under his real name of Jesse James? That is a question we may never know the answer to. One bit of information came to my late mother through Freemason and retired Texas game warden Don Jackson. Mr. Jackson's grandfather was a neighbor to Jesse a.k.a. James L. Courtney in Blevins, Texas, and in Mr. Jackson's family it was passed down that James L. Courtney was Jesse James and that it was a "Masonic Secret."[2]

In Jesse James's diary, he stated that while in Louisiana with his gang (all under aliases, of course, yet coinciding with several robberies in the exact places they had traveled and at the same time), he stayed overnight with a man named Gervais Fontenot. Upon further research I found that Gervais was, at that time, a retired U.S. marshal. Now upon first glance it seems strange that an outlaw would be associating with a U.S. marshal but when one takes into consideration that more than a few Texas Rangers and other lawmen in the Old West had been known to have been outlaws prior, during, and/or after serving as lawmen, it doesn't seem quite as strange. What did shock me when researching Gervais, though, was when I found out that he was the nephew of the infamous pirate Jean Baptiste Lafitte. That's right, Jesse James stayed the night at the home of the nephew of Jean Lafitte, the pirate!

What does that have to do with anything other than an interesting side note? On researching Jean Lafitte, I found that, in the words of The Grand Lodge of the State of Louisiana, "when General Andrew Jackson arrived in New Orleans in 1814 and prepared the city against a British invasion during the end of the War of 1812, he came as a Freemason; attending Lodge with Governor Claiborne and holding masonic communications with pirate Jean Lafitte and his brother, General Dominique You."[3]

It only stands to reason that Jean Lafitte couldn't have had masonic communications with General Andrew Jackson (or anyone other than a Freemason) unless he himself were a Freemason. That is very interesting indeed, and while I have not yet found proof that Gervais, Jean Lafitte's nephew, was a Freemason, he was Lafitte's family and he did host Jesse James for the night while Jesse and his gang were on a robbing spree in Louisiana. With Jean Lafitte being a pirate, and a successful one at that, it definitely lends credence to the idea that Jean Lafitte may have also been involved in the Templar Treasures I wrote about in my first book, *Jesse James and the Lost Templar Treasures*. I would go further to suggest that if Jean Lafitte was involved with the acquisition of and burial of treasures, as Jesse was, and being a Freemason as Jesse was, that the two men were involved in the same activities, namely that of taking gold and other wealth and information and redepositing it for use by someone or some group of people at a later date. I strongly believe that that someone, or group of people, was most likely the Freemasons, thus linking the two famously infamous characters.

Could or would a group like the Freemasons also provide the protection men like Jesse and Lafitte would have needed in order to pull off certain heists and later vanish? In endorsing my first book, Timothy W. Hogan, the current Templar Grand Master, explained that Templar treasure from Jerusalem had been moved to the Americas to help establish a free nation. He wrote, "There have always been those who have sought to shape history to ensure that freedoms and artifacts could be preserved in the Americas." Perhaps Jesse was one of those men.

Hogan's endorsement does a wonderful job of illustrating why men like Jesse James, Jean Lafitte, and others would have buried treasure. They were much more than just mere outlaws or pirates, riding or sailing around robbing people for their own benefit. Their efforts, and the treasures they had obtained, were to be used for a higher purpose and, hard as it may be for some people to believe, that purpose involved helping to secure freedom and liberty, then and now. What's more, it helped to ensure that certain sacred and ancient artifacts were preserved.

In the beginning, research pointed toward the Knights of the Golden Circle, or KGC, the secretive pro-Confederate organization founded in the mid-1850s with the goal of preserving slavery and creating an empire based on agriculture with labor provided by slaves. The KGC were "a secretive organization created in 1854, proposed to establish a slaveholding empire encompassing the southern United States, the West Indies, Mexico, and parts of Central America. Centering on Havana, this empire would be some 2,400 miles in diameter—hence the name Golden Circle. Leaders of the KGC argued that their empire would have a virtual monopoly on the world's supply of tobacco and sugar and perhaps cotton and have the strength to preserve slavery in the South from constant attacks by northern Abolitionists."[4] The group was said to have included men such as Albert Pike, John Wilkes Booth (assassin of President Abraham Lincoln), and Jesse. I have yet to see any evidence that Jesse or Albert Pike were members.

After the American Civil war was over, the KGC were said to have gone underground and began planning ways to fund a second civil war. In doing so, they are said to have been involved in burying vast sums of gold and silver and to have employed the use of a template that would be overlaid on a map and used to locate the treasures later, when needed. This template is usually referred to as a KGC treasure template.

While researching any treasures associated with Jesse James and the KGC, I came across a story of a treasure that had been partially recovered from a small mountain in New Mexico called Victorio Peak by a man named Doc Noss. Some claim this treasure to have been placed there by the KGC, but further research revealed that the treasure likely predated the KGC by several centuries. It is believed by some to have been part of the treasures of Cibola, one of the legendary Seven Cities of Gold searched for by Spanish explorer Francisco Vasquez de Coronado. This treasure hinted at possible connections with the Catholic Church via Pope Pius III. If the connection with Pope Pius III is true, it would date the treasure back to at least the thirteenth century, and if the stories of Cibola have any truth to them, then that could date the treasure back to at least the eighth century. The story of Victorio Peak has something to it as it was mentioned in the Watergate hearings in 1973 when "John Dean, the former lawyer for President Richard M. Nixon, mentioned that Attorney General John Mitchell had been asked to pull strings to allow some searchers to look for the gold."[5]

Another treasure legend said to be connected with this story is that of the Bruton vault at the Bruton Parish Church in Williamsburg, Virginia. In researching the treasure legends of the Bruton vault, Marie Bauer Hall, wife of 33 degree Freemason, author, lecturer, and scholar, Manly Palmer Hall, discovered anagrams on several tombstones in the cemetery at the Bruton Parish Church. Detailing more codes she had found, not only on tombstones but also in books, she connected Sir Francis Bacon to these and essentially painted him as the mastermind responsible for the Bruton vault and other amazing feats. The contents of the vault are said to hold the answers to secrets that would be of great value to both the world in general and to Freemasons.

It seemed the treasures had more in common with Freemasonry and Rosicrucianism than the KGC. I believe Francis Bacon's *New Atlantis, A Worke Unfinished* was written not only as a means of expressing his desire for a free, democratic society and universal education but also as a call to action for like-minded souls. The vehicles by which they chose to accomplish this great work may have been Freemasonry and other associated societies.

The current Bruton Parish Church in Williamsburg, Virginia, was built in 1715. It is 1,715 miles from Victorio Peak, New Mexico, and it's 1,715 feet from the Christopher Wren building located on the campus of the College of William and Mary, founded in 1693 by charter from King William III and Queen Mary II of England. The Christopher Wren building is the oldest college building still in use in America. This is where Marie Bauer Hall discovered her findings. I felt the above information warranted a closer look, especially that number: 1,715.

It was around this time that I learned of three more treasures that had been recovered and was shown where they had been buried. These treasures, along with the others mentioned above, appeared to be connected with the treasure legends I had originally been searching for. I used what was labeled the KGC treasure template and discovered the correct scale to use. Once I knew the dimensions of the template, I overlaid them on a map and found that not only did all of the treasures I had learned of fit the template, but that these various treasures, buried in different parts of North America at different times in history, were connected. The number 1,715 came up frequently, as did others. When I drew a line from Victorio Peak to a large treasure near Georgetown, Texas, that Ms. Callahan from Texas State Attorney General Wagonner Carr's office had shown us, the measurement was 548 miles and the angle of this new line off of the line from Victorio Peak to Williamsburg, Virginia was 33 degrees. Was the number 33 another coincidence? Perhaps. But perhaps not.

Reading about Freemasonry, Albert Pike's book *Morals and Dogma* makes frequent mention of Kabbalah. After more research, which led me into learning about Kabbalah and its various forms (Jewish Kabbalah, Christian Cabala, and Occult Qaballah), I had to wonder if the numbers involved could have some deeper meaning behind them.

I learned that the surname Bacon, as in Francis Bacon, using the alphabet of his day, the Elizabethan alphabet, has a gematria value of 33, which is also the angle off the Victorio Peak-Bruton Parish Church line to Georgetown, Texas. Furthermore, there are 33 degrees in Scottish Rite Freemasonry and the cover of Albert Pike's book is adorned with a double-headed eagle with the number 33 above it. Author Gregory H. Peters writes that the double-headed eagle can be associated with the Kabbalistic Tree of Life, one of the most fundamental symbols of Jewish, Christian, and Occult Kabbalah.

I began working with those numbers that kept showing up repeatedly. The number 1,715 can be translated, when using Hebrew gematria, as "behold, the Tree of Life." The second number I had to work with was 548, the distance between Victorio Peak and the Georgetown site; 548 can be expressed as 4 multiplied by 137. The number 4 can be translated as meaning "door," and 137 is the gematria for the word "Kabbalah."

I believe the treasure Jesse helped to bury has very little, if anything, to do with the KGC for these reasons. Not only does the evidence point to Freemasonry and Rosicrucianism, I found it went back even further. From the discovery of a hidden map on the frontispiece of a sixteenth-century manuscript titled *Portae Lucis,* written by a Jewish Converso by the name of Paolo Riccio, I believe the treasures can be traced through Christian cabbalists, Jewish Kabbalists and rabbis, alchemists, and famous artists with connections going back to the Knights Templar. In other words, Jesse wasn't working for the KGC; he was working for the higher good.

Being a Freemason may have offered Jesse some protection, but it wasn't his only form of protection. The fact is that Jesse was surrounded by former Quantrill's guerillas. Quantrill's guerillas were some of the most feared fighting men during the American Civil War, renowned for their deadly fighting skills and horsemanship. After the Civil War was over, while regular Confederate forces were granted amnesty, Quantrill's guerillas were denied that courtesy and branded as outlaws. They were hunted men, and when caught, they were most often executed. As a result, many former guerillas changed their names and relocated to places like Blevins, Texas, where Jesse had relocated. Some of those former guerillas, such as the Younger brothers and others, turned to outlawry.

Besides being surrounded by Quantrill's guerillas, we believe Jesse was also married to Mary Ellen Barron—the daughter of former Texas Ranger Thomas Hudson Barron—which may have also provided some protection. While traditionally accepted history claims that Jesse James was married to his first cousin Zee Mimms, our family stories along with decades of research show that Jesse never married Zee and was instead married to Mary Ellen Barron in Texas under his alias of James Lafayette Courtney. Our family believes that Zee Mimms was married to Jesse's other first cousin Wood Hite.

That explains how Jesse stayed safe, but what about Billy the Kid? According to the quote in the preceding chapter from Jesse Evans,

Brushy Bill Roberts first denied being Billy the Kid and later admitted that he was Billy the Kid. According to Billy, or Brushy Bill Roberts, he only stole a few cattle and horses in his time and wasn't interested in robbing banks, trains, and stages as Jesse had done. That could be true or it could just be Billy not wanting to incriminate himself. Regardless of what crimes Billy, or Brushy Bill, did or did not want to involve himself in, he was very well connected with some of the most notorious outlaws in the Old West. I find it hard to believe that he wasn't involved more deeply than he claims, although that is possible. The quote below, translated from a website where it had been posted in French, shows that Brushy Bill also stated the following, describing his life while staying at a ranch in Texas:

> My job was generally that of a chore boy around the property. They were gone most of the time, leaving no one behind but Aunt Ann, the black cook, and me. I would take a pack horse and go to the village for provisions and their ammunition. During the time that I was there, I met all the outlaws in the territory. It seemed like a haven for outlaws. I got to know the brothers James and Younger, the Joe Shaw gang, Rube Burrow and Jim Burrow and their gang. I saw them bring bags of money and throw them on the bed and Belle was counting it up, saying, "Here's your share and here's my share." Two men were sitting right there holding their guns [to stand guard]. Once, an outlaw ordered me to saddle his horse and spoke very harshly to me, and Belle surprised him. She told him that I was her kid and that she would protect me.[6]

Belle, mentioned here, is Belle Starr, who we will meet in more detail in the following chapter. In short, she was very friendly with the James-Younger Gang and was even said by some history buffs to have had a great affection for Cole Younger. She knew them during the American Civil War and afterward as they fostered their outlaw career. This shows that Brushy Bill and Jesse James clearly had an acquaintance in common. Belle had a ranch in Bosque County, Texas, near the town of Clifton, which is only roughly forty miles northwest of Jesse's ranch in Blevins, Texas and approximately thirty-three miles east/southeast of Hico, Texas. This ranch wasn't her only property, as she was also known to have stayed in a few other locations, like Briartown, in what is now Oklahoma.

Belle has even possibly been identified in a family photo we have showing Jesse and his family together with Frank James on Frank's wedding day, which they celebrated at Jesse's ranch in Blevins, Texas. This illustrates yet another possible connection between Billy the Kid and Jesse James, one that suggests they were both part of a coordinated network that afforded them some protection and gave them a higher purpose. They lived close enough to help one another but not too close, so as to avoid undue attention or suspicion.

NEW FACES IN
AN OLD PHOTOGRAPH

In the autumn of 2010, my late mother Betty Dorsett Duke was notified of a photograph that included Jesse James; Frank James and his new bride, Annie Ralston; their mother, Zerelda, and step-father, Dr. Rueben Samuel; their sister Susan Parmer; and several of Jesse's neighbors from Blevins, Texas, namely, Joseph Zachariah "J. Z." Jackson and his wife, Harriet; his brother Sol Jackson; and others. The photo was an amazing find, and she was fortunate to have obtained the photo in an auction on eBay. That photo alone proved that Jesse James and his entire family were in Blevins, Texas, during Frank James's wedding to Annie, and my late mother went into great detail about that in her final book, *Jesse James—The Smoking Gun*.

The people in the photograph on the next page, starting with those in the front row, left to right, are:

Frank James (wearing the light-colored suit)
Annie Ralston James (Frank's wife, wearing his hat, with Jesse's hat in her lap)
and Jesse James (the tall man with the dark moustache wearing a dark-colored suit)

In the middle row, left to right, are:

Sara Jackson (wife of Sol Jackson)
Susan James Parmer (Frank and Jesse James's sister)
Zerelda James Samuel (wife of Reuben Samuel and Frank, Jesse, and
   Susan James's mother)
Mary Ellen Barron James (Jesse's wife, second from right)
Harriet Jackson (wife of J. Z. Jackson, far right)

Fig. 5.1. Jesse (front row right), Frank (front row left), Zerelda (behind
Frank), and family and friends in Blevins, Texas.

In the back row are:

Dr. Reuben Samuel (far left, Frank, Jesse, and Susan's stepfather)
Sol Jackson (second from right, neighbor)
J. Z. Jackson (far right, neighbor)

In the beginning we were not sure who the lady in the back row was, fourth from the left. Most everyone else had been identified, and we decided to set the photo aside for a time and take a break from that part of our research. Shortly after taking that break, and while looking into other areas of Jesse's life and associates, the question that had stumped us appeared to have been solved. Not only were Jesse's family and neighbors present at Frank's wedding, but another guest in the photo appears to be none other than Myra Bell Shirley a.k.a. Belle Starr a.k.a. the Bandit Queen!

It is widely known that Belle was in the same part of Texas that Jesse was living in at the time that photograph was taken in 1875. Belle had been arrested in 1875 by Sheriff Lawrence Sullivan "Sul" Ross, who later became governor of Texas, in Waco, Texas.[1]

It is also known that Belle Starr owned property a few miles outside of Clifton, Bosque County, Texas, along a waterway known as "Coon Creek" that flows into the Brazos River approximately twenty-four miles upstream from Waco, Texas. An article in the *Clifton Record* states that "Starr lived in Bosque County for several years with then-husband/outlaw Jim Reed prior to her marriage to Sam Starr."[2] The article goes on to mention how Belle "was murdered in 1889 in Oklahoma. Her killer is still a mystery."[3]

You may be wondering by now just who was Belle Starr, and how does she fit in with Jesse James? Those are very good questions, and I will now divulge that information to you. Belle Starr was born Myra Maybelle Shirley, on February 5, 1848, in Jasper County, Missouri, to John and Elizabeth Hatfield Shirley. Elizabeth, Belle's mother, was related to the Hatfield family who are so well known for the notorious, long, and deadly Hatfield and McCoy feud. In the 1860s, living in Southwestern Missouri (or anywhere along the western border of Missouri) was rough and it got much harder during the American Civil War.

When fighting started, the Shirley family relocated to Texas, but at least one of Belle's siblings, Bud, stayed behind and joined Quantrill's guerillas. Bud was later killed while fighting. It's said that Cole Younger,

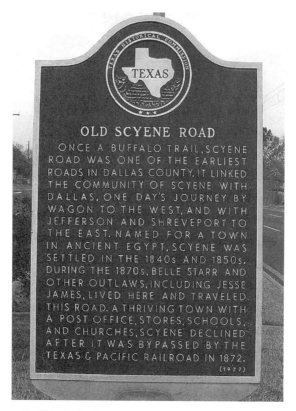

Fig 5.2. Belle Starr and Jesse James mentioned on
a Texas Historical Marker near Dallas, Texas.
Photo by Pleasant Grove and Proud.

the eldest of the Younger brothers and integral part of the James-
Younger Gang after the Civil War was over, traveled to the Shirley
family ranch in Texas to deliver the news of Bud's death. (Others state
that it was Cole Younger who helped move the Shirley family to Texas.)
After the war was over, the James-Younger Gang fled to Texas following a robbery in 1866 and stayed for a time on the Shirley family ranch.
This is when Belle is said to have met her first of possibly four husbands, outlaw and former Quantrill guerilla, James C. "Jim" Reed.[4]

Jim and Belle were married and had two children. During their
marriage, they are said to have stayed for a time in California and even
visited Jesse and Frank at their uncle Drury Woodson James's Paso

Robles spa and resort in that same state.[5] It's said that sometime after the birth of their second child, Jim and Belle parted ways over Jim's having met another woman. Not long afterward in 1874, Jim Reed was shot and killed by a law officer in Paris, Texas.

It's claimed that Belle was married to one of Cole Younger's brothers, Charles Younger, while others believe her to have been married to Bob Younger. "In 1880, Belle married Cole Younger's cousin, Bruce Younger, a petty outlaw who supposedly rode with some famous gangs. This marriage only lasted three weeks. Bruce Younger disappeared into history, but a newspaper account years later identified a mummified body found in a cave in New Mexico as his."[6] Another source puts it differently: "In 1878 Belle Reed appears to have married Bruce Younger, perhaps in Coffeyville, Kansas. If that relationship existed, it soured and she married Samm Starr in the Cherokee Nation on June 5, 1880."[7]

There, she learned ways of organizing, planning and fencing for the rustlers, horse thieves and bootleggers, as well as harboring them from the law. Belle's illegal enterprises proved lucrative enough for her to employ bribery to free her colleagues from the law whenever they were caught.

In 1883, Belle and Sam were arrested by Bass Reeves, charged with horse theft and tried before "The Hanging Judge" Isaac Parker in Fort Smith, Arkansas; the prosecutor was United States Attorney W.H.H. Clayton. She was found guilty and served nine months at the Detroit House of Corrections in Detroit, Michigan. Belle proved to be a model prisoner, and during her time in jail, she won the respect of the prison matron. In contrast, Sam was incorrigible and assigned to hard labor.

In 1886, she eluded conviction on another theft charge, but on December 17, Sam Starr was involved in a gunfight with his cousin Law Officer Frank West. Both men were killed, and Belle's life as an outlaw queen—and what had been the happiest relationship of her life—abruptly ended with her husband's death.[8]

Fig 5.3. Family photo of Belle Starr compared with historical photo of Belle Starr.

Notice the first sentence in the previous quote, where we learn that Belle Starr was adept at organizing, planning, fencing, harboring (providing safe haven for outlaws), and bribery. That bit of information alone says much more about her than meets the eye. One doesn't just jump into that world and make a good living at it if they're just a simple outlaw, riding around shooting their guns and acting wild. That sort of life requires cunning, patience, shrewd intelligence, a lot of nerve, and a calculating mind. It's no wonder she was known in the dime novel arena as "the female Jesse James."[9] And speaking of Jesse, knowing Belle Starr was at his home in Blevins, Texas, and knowing her unique set of skills, it doesn't take much of a stretch of the imagination to see how the services of a lady such as Belle Starr could have come in very handy in a situation where an outlaw such as Jesse James was trying to fake his own death.

After the death of her husband Sam Starr, Belle met another man, fifteen years her junior. This man was a Creek Indian named Jim July. "In 1889, July was arrested for robbery and summoned to Fort Smith, Arkansas, to face charges. Belle accompanied her young lover for part of the journey but turned back before reaching Fort Smith. On her way home, someone ambushed and fatally wounded her with two shotgun blasts to her back. Jim July believed the murderer was a neighbor with whom the couple had been feuding, but no one was ever convicted of the crime."[10] According to another source, the neighbor, Edgar Watson, was a fugitive from Florida with a price on his head for murder.

Belle had been warned by the tribal council that any further harboring of fugitives would earn her expulsion from Younger's Bend. When Edgar A. Watson approached her about renting some land, she eagerly accepted his money, unaware that he was a fugitive. Starr then learned from Watson's wife that the Florida authorities were after him for murder. Concerned with protecting her home, she tried to refund his money, but Watson refused to let her out of the deal. "In a face-to-face confrontation," writes Arnott, "she chided him with a comment that Florida authorities might be interested in his whereabouts." Watson was more than a little angry when he took back his rent money and settled on a nearby farm. He would soon be one among several individuals said to have motive for the murder of Belle Starr.[11]

The epitaph on Belle's headstone reads as follows:

BELLE STARR

Born in Carthage, Missouri
February 5, 1848
Died February 3, 1889
Shed not for her the bitter tear
Nor give the heart to vain regret,
Tis but the casket that lies here,
The gem that filled it sparkles yet

Fig 5.4. Belle Starr and fellow outlaw
Blue Duck a.k.a. Bluford Duck.

While many of the details of Belle's life are not known, it is known that she definitely had connections with Jesse James, Cole Younger, and many other outlaws. The quote in the previous chapter, from Brushy Bill Roberts a.k.a. Billy the Kid, also made mention of her (p. 37). Add that to the photograph of Frank James's wedding taken with Jesse and their families, friends, and neighbors in Blevins, Texas, and it is glaringly obvious to me that they were very well acquainted.

Like Jesse James, the Younger brothers, and other figures in that part of the world at that time in history, Belle Starr, if not for the Civil War, could have gone on to have been an outstanding figure in society. Together, Belle and these other characters had great intelligence and

Fig 5.5. Belle Starr in Fort Smith, Arkansas, circa 1886.

bravery, were loyal to those around them, and seemed to have been very shrewd in their business dealings. Their connections with powerful people, the relationships between these families, and their likely connection to larger networks like the Freemasons piqued my curiosity and drove me to want to dig much deeper. They were much more than mere outlaws or ruffians, much more than what we see at first glance or what most history books have revealed. Much like many early-day Texas Rangers and other lawmen around the world during rough times in a nation's history, outlaws of the Wild West rode (and often crossed well beyond) a fine line—the line between hero and villain.

FAMILY TIES

There were several powerful connections and family ties that Jesse James and his peers shared, on a local level, with those who were involved in government and the law, as well as with all of those who were allegedly trying to capture Jesse James and his gang.

Jesse James left many clues as to his true identity. Among those clues are his diaries and treasure maps, which have yielded a wealth of information over the years as to who he was, who he was related to, and who he knew. One obvious clue was the line shared earlier from his diary, in which he wrote "when stemm and tryst, James L. Courtney is my heist." It seems obvious from that statement that he was admitting that he stole the name of James L. Courtney. In addition to that piece of information, even though he was operating under the alias James L. Courtney, he also signed his diary JWJ and J. James (JWJ being interpreted as being the initials of Jesse's full name, Jesse Woodson James).

Researchers into Jesse's life have found that both Jesse Woodson James and the real James L. Courtney were related in various ways.

One of those relations ties back to Sarah E. Mason Barbee James, whom Jesse descended from as follows: Sarah Mason Barbee married Thomas James in 1699. Their son Captain John James married Dinah Allen in 1738,[1] and their son, Rev. John M. James, married Mary Polly Poor in 1790.[2] Their son, Rev. Robert Sallee James, mar-

48

ried Zerelda E. Cole in 1825 in Kentucky. Their son was Jesse Woodson James.

As it turns out, the real James L. Courtney also descends from Sarah Mason Barbee James as follows: Andrew Barbee* married Sarah Elizabeth Mason and their son Thomas Barbee married Margaret Williams. Their daughter Mary Barbee (b. 1727) married William F. Courtney and their son James Courtney married Sarah Kesterson. James Courtney and Sarah Kesterson's son George Washington Courtney (born around 1780) married Elizabeth Ensor (b. 1788) and their son was Stephen Courtney (b. 1822). Stephen Courtney used the alias of Andrew Jackson Haun. Stephen a.k.a. Andrew married Dinah Courtney a.k.a. Dinah Haun. Their son was the real James L. Courtney who may have married a woman by the name of Susan Eubanks.

The real James L. Courtney's great-great-grandfather was William Francis Courtney, who married Mary Barbee. Mary was the granddaughter of Andrew Barbee and Sarah Mason Barbee.[3] After Andrew Barbee's death, Sarah married Thomas James, Jesse James's direct ancestor, and that is when she became Sarah Mason Barbee James.

The Barbees of Clay County, Missouri (the same county Jesse James was born and raised in) were also related to Jesse James. The Barbees connect to the real James L. Courtney's family in Clay County through Charles Mortimer Barbee born 13 Nov 1817 in Georgetown, Kentucky and died 5 Feb 1896 in Liberty, Clay County, Missouri. Charles married Mary Jane Estes on 24 Nov 1857 in Liberty.

---

*The Andrew Barbee who married Sarah Elizabeth Mason should not be confused with his and Sarah's great-grandson, Andrew Barbee born in 1767, son of John Barbee and Phyllis Duncan. The younger Andrew Barbee married Rebecca Margaret Bradford, daughter of John "Old Wisdom" Bradford and Elizabeth James. Elizabeth James was the daughter of Captain John James and Dinah Allen. (Complied by Edmund West. Individual Family Records Family Data Collection of Ancestry.com)

This information places my Barbee family living in Clay County, Missouri as of 1857, seven years after Robert [Jesse's father] left for California. Zerelda would have already been married to Reuben Samuel [Jesse's stepfather]. Charles Mortimer Barbee is the son of Nathaniel Barbee and Catherine Bradford. Nathaniel Barbee was the son of Joseph Barbee and Nancy Ann Withers. Joseph Barbee was the son of Andrew Barbee and Jane Delany.

Andrew Barbee was the son of Thomas Barbee and Margaret Williams as well as the brother of Mary Barbee who married William F. Courtney. Thomas Barbee was the son of Andrew Barbee and Sarah Elizabeth Mason. Sarah later married Thomas James and they became the founders of the James family of America.[4]

Jesse had many connections through family to powerful or well-known people in his day and afterward. One of his relatives was the very governor of Missouri who was allegedly trying to catch Jesse and his gang. Governor Thomas T. Crittenden, governor of Missouri from 1881 to 1885, was related to Jesse and Frank James through the governor's uncle, John Jordan Crittenden.[5]

Another such connection was Sheriff James H. Timberlake, who arrested the Ford boys after they claimed to have assassinated Jesse James and was allegedly trying to capture Jesse and Frank. Sherriff Timberlake was married to Elizabeth Thomason, daughter of Grafton Thomason and granddaughter of Samuel Thomason, Jr.[6] Samuel's son, Robert Thomason, married Sarah "Sallie" Lindsay Cole, the mother of Zerelda Cole Frank and the maternal grandmother of Frank and Jesse James.[7]

Sheriff Timberlake also strongly denied that Frank James had attended Jesse's funeral, yet Frank was clearly present in a recently discovered photo (fig. 6.1). So, if Timberlake would lie and cover for Frank, it seems logical that he would just as easily have lied for Jesse.

Another interesting relation to Jesse James is a famous outlaw couple, Bonnie and Clyde. Yes, we were just as shocked as you when

Fig. 6.1. My family's interpretation of the photo showing those in attendance at Jesse's alleged funeral. In my book *The Mysterious Life and Faked Death of Jesse James*, I showed how the man on the far right might be Jesse himself.

we first discovered this! Bonnie Parker's maternal grandfather owned a farm next door to Jesse James a.k.a. James L. Courtney in Blevins, Texas. Furthermore, Bonnie's uncle was Henry Jackson Mims of Sabine Parish, Louisiana.

Now, traditional history claims that Jesse Woodson James married his first cousin, Zee Mimms, which my family's oral tradition and subsequent research over the last few decades has proven to have been false. Zee Mimms was first cousins with Jesse James and she did marry her first cousin, but the cousin she married was Wood Hite. Wood Hite was the man killed and passed off as Jesse James in Missouri in 1882.

I emailed a man by the name of Ray Holt who had information

on his RootsWeb page, an online host for family trees and part of the WorldConnect Project, and asked him if he knew whether or not his Mims were related to the Mimms in Missouri who were related to the James family. He replied: "They are connected. Zee would be a distant cousin of my Mims."[8]

Bonnie's beau, Clyde C. Barrow, also has a potential Blevins, Texas, connection. His grandmother was Mahala Ann Barron. The last name *Barron* should sound familiar as we believe Jesse's wife was Mary Ellen Barron. Her father was former Texas Ranger Captain Thomas Hudson Barron of Blevins, Texas. The late genealogist Carol Holmes explains:

Mahala Barron was married to William Wilson Walker and their daughter, Cumi Walker, was the mother of Clyde Chesnut Barrow. Mahala Ann Barron is the daughter of Samuel B. Barron and Phoebe Barber/Barbee. Samuel B. Barron was born in 1808 in Georgia and Thomas Hudson Barron was born 1796 in Kentucky. Thomas Hudson Barron family can be found in Charles County, Maryland and tie into the Lindsey family who Jesse's mother Zerelda descends from. Mahala Barron has family ties to the Lindsey family and many of the names associated with those of Thomas Hudson Barron.

History of the Barron Family: John Barron came from Ireland. In this family were Thomas and Teresa. John Barron lived near Elizabeth Town, Kentucky, and married Sarah Tweedell of Virginia. John Barron was a farmer. In this union were Joseph, Benjamin, Matthew, Martha, Mary, Harrison, Jinken Rogers, Thomas, Susan, David & Miles. They moved from KY to Sangamon Co, Illinois, later moving to Astoria, Fulton Co., Illinois.

Jesse James's Lindsey family, as well as the Barron's Lindsey family, were in Charles Co. Maryland at the same time. The James, Barrons (also known as Barns and Barrow, Barber/Barbee) and the Wilson/Walker family all connect to one another.

A man living in Blevins, Texas from 1871 until the day he died under the name of Courtney to protect the traditional story that Jesse W. James lived and died in Missouri, reflects another part of the mystery about a little girl by the name of Bonnie Parker. To explain the Mims family connection to Blevins, Texas is quite amazing.[9]

I know all of the surnames can be confusing at times. To try to put it in simpler terms, Clyde Barrow, of Bonnie and Clyde fame/notoriety, was the grandson of Mahala Barron. That Barron line connects to the Lindsey family. Jesse James's mother is descended from that same Lindsey family. Jesse married Mary Ellen Barron and Mary Ellen's Barron family also connects to that same Lindsey family. So Clyde Barrow and Mary Ellen Barron are both related not only to one another but also to Jesse James.

Also of note regarding the Bonnie and Clyde connections is that along with one of the treasure maps, there was a small clipping from a newspaper handed down through the family. When we first received the map and newspaper clipping, we wondered, why would an article about Bonnie and Clyde be included with that map? Now we know why.

On the following pages, among some of the names highlighted, are relations of Jesse James through blood and marriage to various figures such as Billie Sol Estes; U.S. President Lyndon Baines Johnson; R. E. B. Baylor, a Baptist leader and lawyer who was the namesake of Baylor University in Waco, Texas; other Baylor and Bledsoe families; Sheriff Timberlake; Missouri Governor Crittenden; Police Commissioner H. H. Craig, who had also been involved in allegedly trying to capture Jesse James; and many others.

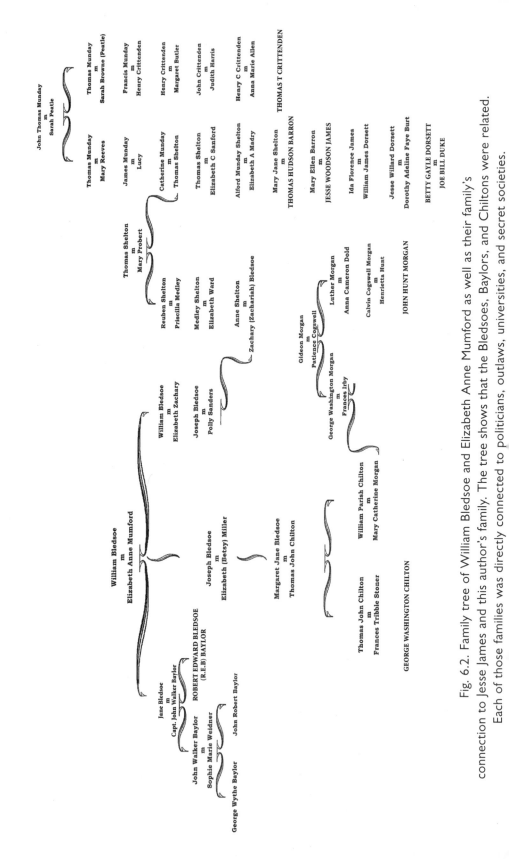

Fig. 6.2. Family tree of William Bledsoe and Elizabeth Anne Mumford as well as their family's connection to Jesse James and this author's family. The tree shows that the Bledsoes, Baylors, and Chiltons were related. Each of those families was directly connected to politicians, outlaws, universities, and secret societies.

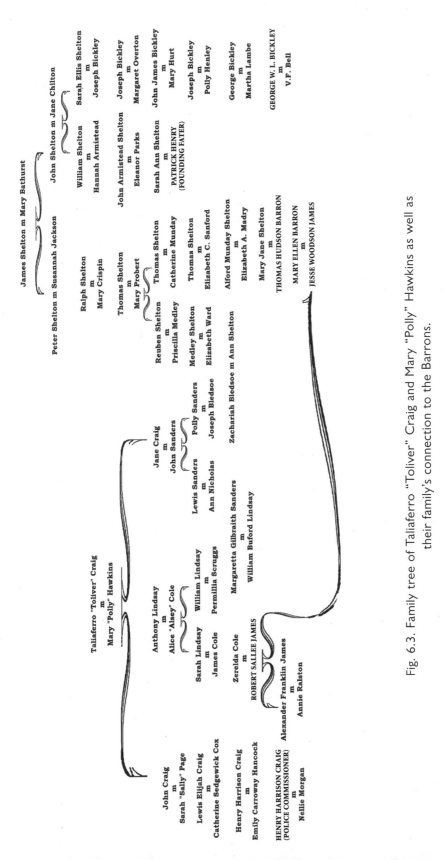

Fig. 6.3. Family tree of Taliaferro "Toliver" Craig and Mary "Polly" Hawkins as well as their family's connection to the Barrons.

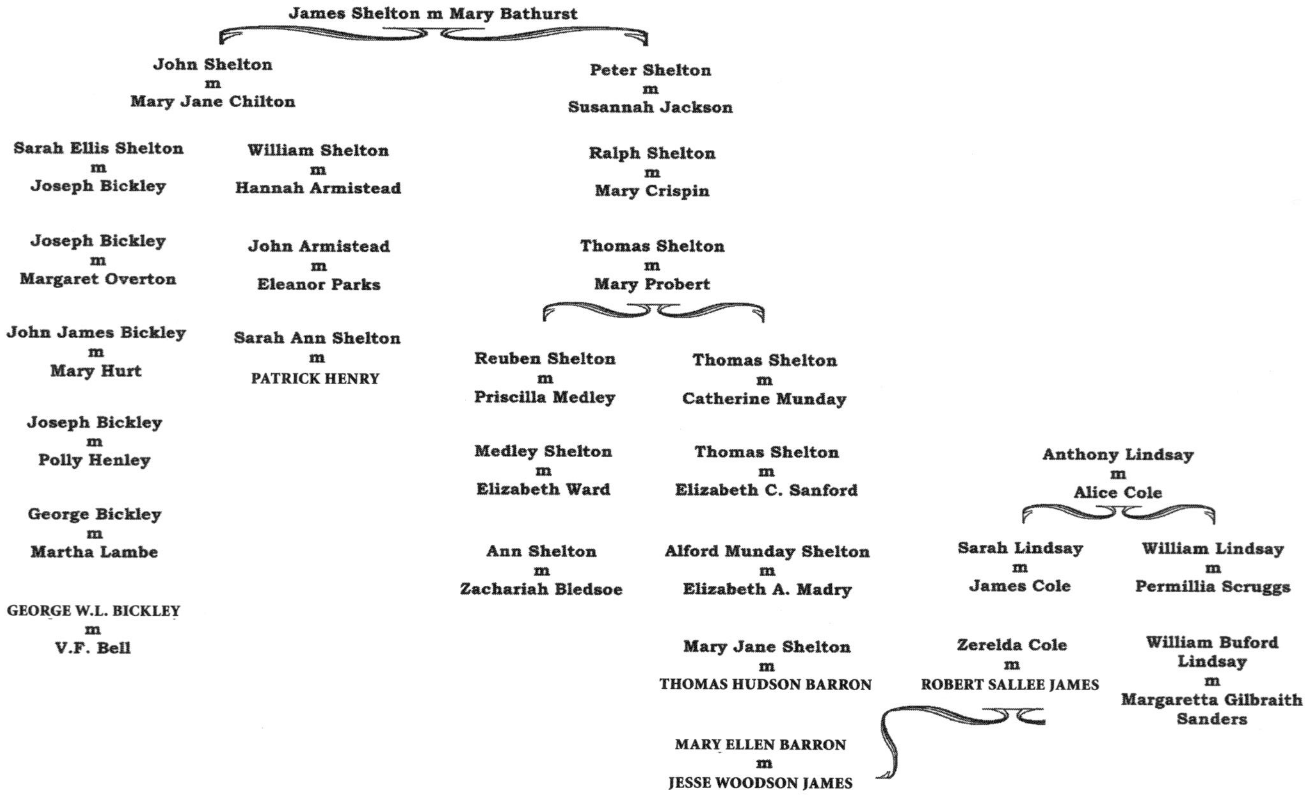

James Shelton m Mary Bathurst

John Shelton
m
Mary Jane Chilton

Peter Shelton
m
Susannah Jackson

William Shelton
m
Hannah Armistead

Ralph Shelton
m
Mary Crispin

John Armistead
m
Eleanor Parks

Thomas Shelton
m
Mary Probert

Sarah Ann Shelton
m
PATRICK HENRY

Sarah Ellis Shelton
m
Joseph Bickley

Joseph Bickley
m
Margaret Overton

John James Bickley
m
Mary Hurt

Reuben Shelton
m
Priscilla Medley

Thomas Shelton
m
Catherine Munday

Joseph Bickley
m
Polly Henley

Medley Shelton
m
Elizabeth Ward

Thomas Shelton
m
Elizabeth C. Sanford

Anthony Lindsay
m
Alice Cole

George Bickley

Ann Shelton
m
Zachariah Bledsoe

Alford Munday Shelton
m
Elizabeth A. Madry

Sarah Lindsay
m
James Cole

William Lindsay
m
Permillia Scruggs

GEORGE W.L. BICKLEY
m
V.F. Bell

Martha Lambe

Mary Jane Shelton
m
THOMAS HUDSON BARRON

Zerelda Cole
m
ROBERT SALLEE JAMES

William Buford
Lindsay
m
Margaretta Gilbraith
Sanders

MARY ELLEN BARRON
m
JESSE WOODSON JAMES

Fig. 6.4. Family tree of James Shelton and Mary Bathurst as well as their family's connection to the Barrons.

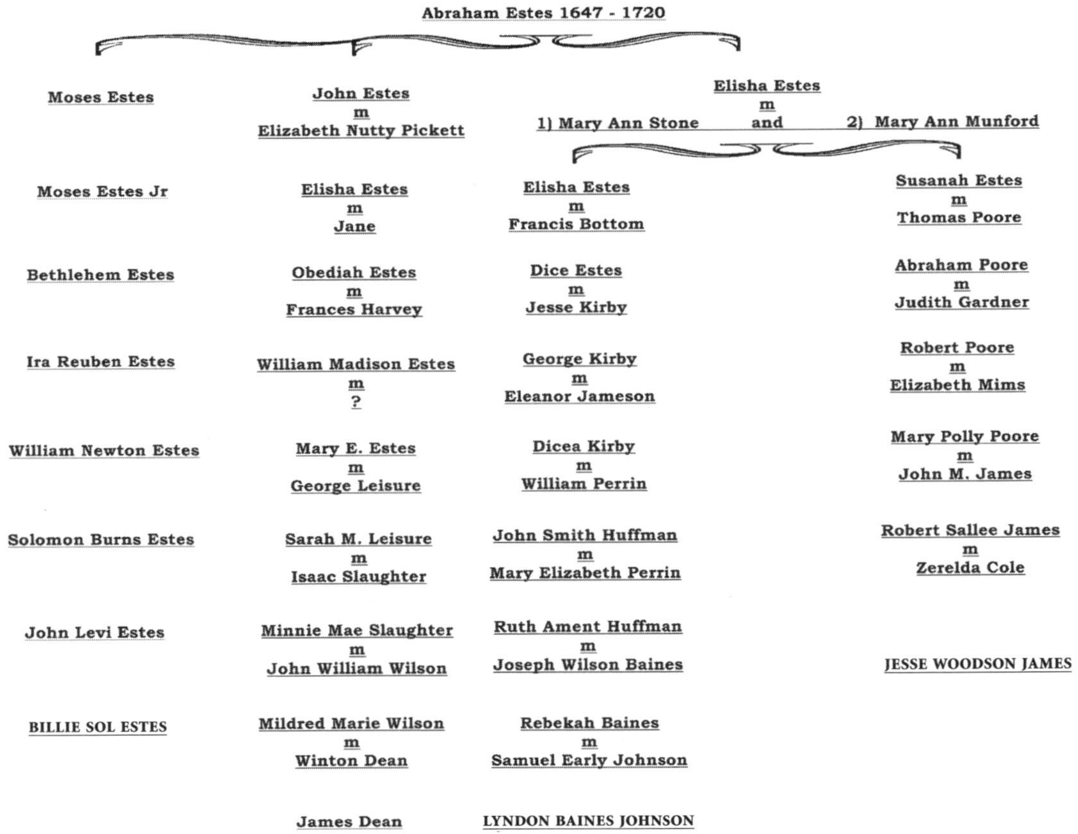

Abraham Estes 1647 - 1720

Elisha Estes

1) Mary Ann Stone   m   and   2) Mary Ann Munford

Moses Estes	John Estes m Elizabeth Nutty Pickett		

1) Mary Ann Stone line:

Moses Estes Jr — Elisha Estes m Francis Bottom — Elisha Estes m Jane

Bethlehem Estes — Dice Estes m Jesse Kirby — Obediah Estes m Frances Harvey

Ira Reuben Estes — George Kirby m Eleanor Jameson — William Madison Estes m ?

William Newton Estes — Dicea Kirby m William Perrin — Mary E. Estes m George Leisure

Solomon Burns Estes — John Smith Huffman m Mary Elizabeth Perrin — Sarah M. Leisure m Isaac Slaughter

John Levi Estes — Ruth Ament Huffman m Joseph Wilson Baines — Minnie Mae Slaughter m John William Wilson

BILLIE SOL ESTES — Rebekah Baines m Samuel Early Johnson — Mildred Marie Wilson m Winton Dean

— LYNDON BAINES JOHNSON — James Dean

2) Mary Ann Munford line:

Susanah Estes m Thomas Poore

Abraham Poore m Judith Gardner

Robert Poore m Elizabeth Mims

Mary Polly Poore m John M. James

Robert Sallee James m Zerelda Cole

JESSE WOODSON JAMES

Fig. 6.5. Family tree of Abraham Estes showing his connection to Billie Sol Estes, Lyndon Baines Johnson, and Jesse James.

WITH FAITH COMES POWER

S ome names survive in our national consciousness as time ticks by. Sometimes, as with Jesse James, we remember those names associated with notoriety; other times, we remember those names associated with good deeds. Sometimes, though, people are both good and bad, or do bad things for a good reason. In this chapter, we'll explore Jesse's connections to influential men of his time—men with names like Baylor, Bledsoe, Chilton, Bickley, and Valindigham. (Admittedly, these names might be most familiar to Texans, but all these families had a large reach in Jesse's time, and that reach extends into our time as well.) The interactions between Jesse and these men illustrate how politics benefited from the outlaws' careers and that these outlaws actually served a higher purpose than just riding around robbing people.

Through researching Jesse James, I found connections not only among Jesse, Billy the Kid, and other outlaws of the Old West, but also among powerful political families, colleges, and even the Baptist church. All of these share a common denominator, which on the surface appears to be Freemasonry but goes even deeper than that.

In the previous chapter I showed how Jesse James is connected to various other families through blood and marriage. These families include the Baylor and Bledsoe families and even several other names, such as Chilton, Bickley, and Valindigham, who played large roles in the shadowy group known as the Knights of the Golden Circle. I'll now show you why that is important and give you an overview of those mentioned above.

Jesse James's father, Robert Sallee James, was a Baptist minister and cofounder of the William Jewell College in Liberty, Missouri. Jesse, using his alias of James L. Courtney, was a Freemason who also supported the Little Deer Creek Baptist Church, of which he was a member and their delegate to the Waco Baptist Association in 1884. But Jesse was seen holding a birthday party for one of his children, and when music was played the children danced. That dancing resulted in Jesse no longer being allowed to attend his church as it was against the church's rules. While the Baptist church Jesse belonged to wouldn't let him attend, he still stood outside the church during services because, according to family legend, he loved hearing the choir sing. Even though that church kicked him out, years later he helped build a new one after it burned down and even moved it to a more suitable location.

"Although many Americans assume that religious participation has declined in America, Finke and Stark present a different picture. In 1776, fewer than 1 in 5 Americans were active in church affairs. Today, church membership includes about 6 out of 10 people."[1] I feel the previous quote illustrates the motivation for various churches to try to gain congregants; whether intentional or not, when those measures were successful, more followers led to a more powerful church. Power can do strange things to people and, in the name of growth, even ecclesiastical and well-meaning people can become tainted by corruption. When viewing the various denominations of protestant churches in early American history, it is not hard to start viewing them as competing corporate entities, each vying with the other for more congregants. Two of the larger upstart denominations were the Methodist and Baptist churches. Both were streamlined and ready to expand. They didn't require hefty donations, and it didn't take their ministers years of intense study to become a minister. Doing so mostly required faith and a willingness to rough it. This suited the two denominations well in a growing nation in the eighteenth and nineteenth centuries. Ministers would ride a circuit and preach in the towns or villages in which they stayed, then pack up and move on. It was also attractive to the ministers as they didn't fall under strict guidelines. All they needed was faith. "Methodist growth was most dramatic—from 2.5 percent of the church going population in 1776 to 34.2 percent in 1850. This made them by far the largest religious body in the nation and the most extensive national institution other than the Federal government. By the middle of the nineteenth century, Methodists boasted 4,000 itinerants, almost 8,000 local preachers and over one million members."[2] But their popularity did not last, and the Baptists overtook them by the end of the 1800s. "Before 1840 and during their meteoric rise, the Methodists had virtually no college-educated clergy among their thousands of circuit riders and local preachers."[3] How did their strength become their downfall? "Their relative slump began at the same time that their amateur clergy were replaced by seminary-educated professionals who claimed episcopal authority over their congregations."[4]

What does that matter? In terms of faith, Baptists, Methodists, and others seem to have wanted more control over how their country was being run and felt any choices they made were aligned with the will of God. With a large and growing congregation, they stood to wield a sizeable portion of political clout, which gave them power. By the end of the nineteenth century, the various Baptist churches across America wielded that political power and used it to their advantage.

One of those early-day Baptist ministers was the Reverend Joseph Bledsoe, "the founder and first pastor of Gilberts Creek Church of Separate Baptists, in Garrard County, Kentucky."[5] The Reverend Joseph Bledsoe fathered quite a few children as was common in that time. Among those children were Jane Bledsoe and Margaret Jane Bledsoe. Jane Bledsoe married Captain John Walker Baylor and Margaret Jane Bledsoe married the Reverend Thomas John Chilton.[6] Jane and

Captain John Baylor were the parents of Robert Emmett Bledsoe Baylor a.k.a. R. E. B. Baylor, the namesake of Baylor University in Waco, Texas.

R. E. B. Baylor, lawyer, college founder, and Baptist leader, was born in Lincoln County, Kentucky, on May 10, 1793, the son of Walker and Jane (Bledsoe) Baylor. His father had been a captain in the Continental Army during the American Revolution, in a company of dragoons that often assisted George Washington. Baylor received his formal education at a country school and at academies around Paris, Kentucky. After service in the War of 1812 he studied law in the office of his uncle, Judge Jesse Bledsoe, and was elected in 1819 to the Kentucky legislature. Around 1820 he moved to Tuscaloosa, Alabama, where he practiced law. In 1824–25 he served in the Alabama legislature. He was elected a representative from Alabama to the Twenty-first Congress of the United States in 1829 and was defeated in the election of 1831. In 1833 he moved to Dallas County, Alabama. Baylor raised a few volunteers and served as a lieutenant colonel against the Creek Indians in Alabama in 1836.

R. E. B. Baylor was converted in 1839 during a Baptist revival meeting conducted by his cousin Thomas Chilton at Talladega, Alabama. The same year he was ordained a Baptist minister and, at the age of forty-six, went to Texas. He settled near La Grange in Fayette County and organized a school. He assisted in the organization of the Union Baptist Association in 1840 and the Texas Baptist Education Society around 1841. With two other Baptist ministers, Z. N. Morrell and Thomas W. Cox, he served under Edward Burleson at the battle of Plum Creek in 1840.[7]

R. E. B. Baylor served as a judge in Waco, Texas, when Waco was a new town. Serving as his court clerk was War of 1812 veteran and Texas Ranger Captain Thomas Hudson Barron, my great-great-great-grandfather. Thomas Hudson Barron fathered twenty-two children during his life, one of which was named Mary Ellen Barron. Mary Ellen married my great-great-grandfather, the infamous outlaw Jesse James, on October 31, 1871. At the time, Jesse was using the alias he borrowed from a cousin, James Lafayette Courtney.

But the connections don't stop there. R. E. B. Baylor's cousin, Margaret Jane Bledsoe, married the Reverend Thomas John Chilton and they had a son, Thomas Chilton, who was born in 1798. Later in life the younger Thomas Chilton married Frances Tribble Stoner, and he was a "U.S. Representative from Kentucky, a prominent Baptist clergyman, and the ghost writer of David Crockett's autobiography."[8] And this, in turn, leads us to the son of Thomas and Frances, George W. Chilton. "George William Chilton, Confederate Army officer, was born to Thomas Chilton and Francis Tribble Stoner on June 4, 1828, in Elizabethtown, Kentucky. He briefly attended Howard College at Marion, Alabama, but with the outbreak of the Mexican War he enlisted as a private in Capt. Christopher B. Acklin's Company B of Col. John C. Hays's First Regiment, Texas Mounted Rifles. After being discharged on September 13, 1846, he returned to Alabama, where he was admitted to the bar in 1848 and set up practice in Talladega. Chilton moved to Texas in 1851 and became an attorney in Tyler. The following year he married Ella Goodman of Tyler; the couple had two children. Chilton was a fiery orator, a member of the Knights of the Golden Circle, and outspoken in his proslavery beliefs."[9] It has been said that George W. Chilton was second in command for the KGC in Texas.

Much has been and is said about the KGC being a secret society, which they were, and rumors abound about the group buying treasures throughout the South and other parts of the country, with some claiming they buried treasures in Mexico and even as far north as Canada.

It is even claimed that the 33rd degree Freemason Albert Pike and Jesse James were high-ranking members of the KGC. I have yet to see any proof of that. Both Albert Pike and Jesse James did fight for the Confederacy during the American Civil War, and it wouldn't shock me to find that they may have been members, or at least had some associations with the group, during the war; but as stated above, I have found no proof of that. Oftentimes people will notice medals or medallions worn by people in those days and attribute that to their being members of the KGC, but in reality, those medallions or other objects or symbols could have been attributed to Freemasonry, as many other secret societies oftentimes patterned or tried to pattern themselves after Freemasonry. "Victory by the Union in the Civil War destroyed the cause for which the KGC had been created and, therefore, ended its life. Bickley [detailed below], who served as a surgeon in the Confederate Army before being arrested as a spy in Indiana in July 1863 and held until October 1865, died in August 1867. Reports of KGC activity circulated for a few more years, but there is no dependable evidence that the organization survived the war in any meaningful way. Perhaps the greatest historical significance that can be assigned to the KGC is its contribution to creating the emotional excitement necessary to persuading southerners to rebel against the United States."[10]

But now that we're talking about the KGC, I think it's the perfect time to mention yet another relative of the families listed above: George Washington Lafayette Bickley, founder of the KGC. George Bickley moved from Cincinnati in the late 1850s under a looming cloud of financial woes. He lobbied various politicians and other influential people, pushing his plan to seize Mexico in an attempt to gain a new territory for slavery. Bickley's failure to bring his plans to fruition resulted in his expulsion from the KGC, to which he was later reinstated. With rumblings of a Civil War after Abraham Lincoln was elected, Bickley and many of his supporters found a new crusade with the secessionist movement. In late 1863, the KGC was reorganized as the Order of American Knights, and again, early in 1864, as the Order of the Sons of Liberty. At this time Clement Laird Vallandigham, the most prominent of the Copperheads, was the organization's supreme commander, but, with growing Union victories, it dissolved in 1864.[11]

Clement Laird Vallandigham, mentioned above, was what is known as a "peacetime Democrat," and peacetime Democrats were also known

as Copperheads. Vallandigham was the head of the Copperhead movement, which was later allied with the KGC. Among their ranks was
a character by the name of Henry Clay Dean, to whom author Mark
Twain referred in his memoir *Life on the Mississipi* as follows:

> He began life poor and without education. But he educated
> himself—on the curbstones of Keokuk. He would sit down on a
> curbstone with his book, careless or unconscious of the clatter of
> commerce and the tramp of the passing crowds, and bury himself in
> his studies by the hour, never changing his position except to draw
> in his knees now and then to let a dray pass unobstructed; and when
> his book was finished, its contents, however abstruse, had been
> burned into his memory, and were his permanent possession. In
> this way he acquired a vast hoard of all sorts of learning, and had it
> pigeonholed in his head where he could put his intellectual hand on
> it whenever it was wanted. His clothes differed in no respect from
> a "wharf-rat's," except that they were raggeder, more ill-assorted and
> inharmonious (and therefore more extravagantly picturesque), and
> several layers dirtier. Nobody could infer the master-mind in the top
> of that edifice from the edifice itself.
>
> He was an orator—by nature in the first place, and later by the
> training of experience and practice. When he was out on a canvass,
> his name was a lodestone which drew the farmers to his stump from
> fifty miles around. His theme was always politics. He used no notes,
> for a volcano does not need notes.[12]

In 1871, whether it was intentional or not, Dean was instrumental in helping the James-Younger Gang rob the Ocobock Brothers
Bank in Corydon, Iowa. Henry Clay Dean was in Corydon to give a
speech in support of a railroad that was to be built through that area.
The Ocobock Brothers, who owned the Ocobock Bank, did not support the idea of the railroad and wouldn't part with any much-needed
donations. Mr. Dean went to the opposite side of the town from the

bank and started his speech. As Mark Twain had stated, Mr. Dean, with his fiery speeches, could draw listeners from miles away, so it is very likely the town was suitably distracted and gathered around to listen. As the speech was underway, the James-Younger Gang rode into Corydon, and several of the members, including Jesse, went inside while others remained outside, keeping watch along the streets. They walked in, took the money, and sauntered away. They were so confident in themselves that they slowly rode by the crowd listening to the speech, and Jesse is said to have proclaimed that their bank had just been robbed. People turned and hushed him, irritated that he interrupted the speech. Jesse and the gang rode away, and I would imagine that had to have been one of the easiest bank robberies that they had pulled off.

Adding fuel to the theory that Henry Clay Dean was connected to the James brothers is the fact that Mr. Dean was well acquainted with Frank James, as is evidenced by his visiting Frank in jail over twelve years later, during the trial where Frank was acquitted of all charges against him. In the article titled "Henry Clay Dean" we read that "Henry Clay Dean returned from Independence this morning. Where he visited Frank James. He denies most emphatically the story that the imprisoned bandit is living in luxury, as has been repeatedly stated. Mr. Dean says that he measured Frank James' cell and that it is just about nine feet by seven in dimensions. There is no brussels carpet, but merely a strip of common carpet covering part of the floor. The bed is little, narrow and apparently not very soft. Mr. Dean says that the whole furniture of the cell would not bring $5 if offered for sale."[13]

Also showing that Mr. Dean was well acquainted with Frank James, the following information regards Frank's 1883 trial for murder and robbery at Gallatin, Missouri (of which he was acquitted): "Late arrivals at Gallatin on Wednesday were Henry Clay Dean, who was expected to make opening remarks for the defense; General Shelby, who registered at the Palace Hotel; and Clifford Saunders, newsman for the St. Louis Post-Dispatch."[14]

Now to attempt to wrap that all into one tidy summary. The Baylor, Bickley, Bledsoe, Chilton, Crittenden, Timberlake, and James families were all interrelated through marriage or blood. Most were cousins, and many of those I mentioned above served their communities and their churches in various ways. The common denominators in this, other than familial relations, are the Baptist church and the locations in which these families lived. These families moved from Kentucky to Missouri and Texas. They served the same side during the American Civil War; while some were more radical than others and didn't even necessarily hold the same political beliefs, other than fighting for the state or community in which they lived, they did serve the same side and they were family. One example of a difference in beliefs can be described by how Mr. Chilton viewed other races versus the way Jesse James and his fellow Quantrill's guerillas treated an African American freedman by the name of John Noland. John Noland served as a scout for Quantrill. "Noland tried to attend most of the reunions and was popular among other Quantrill veterans, who described him as 'a man among men.'"[15]

But what else could have tied them together and led them toward a common yet secretive goal, and why? Was the KGC more involved in this story than I had previously believed?

BURIED TREASURE

We know now of the familial ties and connections with the growth and leadership of the Baptist church and colleges associated with the denomination in the United States. It goes further, and the rest of that story involves legends of buried treasure, Jesse James, and the attempted recovery of that treasure that was alleged to have been funded by Baylor University.

I'll start with a newspaper article from 1992 titled "A New James Gang Digs for Jesse James Safe." The article tells of treasure hunters who searched for an alleged twelve-ton safe, buried over thirty feet deep in the sandy soil not far from the Brazos River in what today is actually Bellmead, Texas. "Using high-tech electronic gear, diggers spotted a 6.5-foot-wide, 6.5-foot-tall and 3.5-foot-deep metal object thought to be the 75-year-old safe stuck in a shale floor under 32 feet of mud in a vacant lot near the Brazos River."[1] The article goes on to describe that the treasure hunters were not able to recover the alleged safe as they were plagued with rain and other misfortunes. Their hunt was abandoned but the legend continued to pique the interest of others, including myself and my late mother, Betty Dorsett Duke. After interviewing Dewey Millay, the owner of the property where this dig had happened, we were informed that the alleged safe contained not only large quantities of gold and jewels, but also documents that included the locations of twelve additional treasures across North America, for a total of thirteen treasure caches. The origin of the story was from a well-known character in the past who claimed to be Jesse James, but was actually a man named J. Frank Dalton. Although it had been proven that Mr. Dalton was not Jesse James, he did have some credible information relating to treasure sites in other locations, and he likely had contact with the James-Younger Gang at various times in his past. Mr. Millay, the property owner, went on to describe to us Dalton's version of how the alleged treasure had come to be there. The safe was delivered via train, and in fact the remnants of a spur from the main railroad track were still visible at the time of our interview. He said the gang buried the safe, and while in the process of doing so, one of the cables snapped, injuring one of the men and causing the safe to crash through some of its subsurface support beams, which was why he said the treasure sank to such a depth. The sandy soils so close to the Brazos River are oftentimes flooded with water just below the surface, and that makes the search much more perilous.

When we met with Dewey Millay on the location he claimed held the safe full of treasure, he had workers excavating the site with large construction equipment, including a backhoe, coffer dams, and two trucks used for liquification and removal of soil. I'm sure it had taken a lot to get this done in terms of money and time, not to mention permits to run the liquified soil and water into the storm drains nearby.

Dewey Millay also pointed to a headstone in Greenwood Cemetery, which was just across the street from the treasure site, that had on the top of it a Masonic square and compasses design. He said this pointed to the location of the buried safe. Stories involving treasure oftentimes seem to come right out of the same imaginations used to create exciting movies, and this one had those same characteristics. That said, it didn't mean it wasn't true, but deserved more research in my opinion.

Several weeks later, once Mr. Millay and his men had completed their excavation and treasure hunt, I returned to the cemetery. While there, my mother and I were looking around for any clues we could find, and we noticed a man at the treasure site across the street. He was watching us and finally approached. He said he was one of the laborers on that treasure dig and that they didn't recover anything. We asked him who was footing the bill for all of that work and all he would say was "Baylor University." I asked his name and he wouldn't give his last name, only his first.

I was once told by an old man that when looking for treasure, it can pay to notice things that seem out of place. While exploring the cemetery and the surrounding area for anything that may have been out of place, I was surprised to have stumbled upon an old headstone. While this headstone was not the same headstone Mr. Millay had pointed out—it was on the opposite side of the same cemetery—this headstone seemed to fit that description. It seemed out of place, and I was reminded of Mr. Millay's comment. This headstone was aligned differently from all of the others, and instead of facing northeast like most of the graves in that cemetery, this one was facing in a more easterly direction, enough so to be noticeably out of line with the others around it. It was tucked in a corner of the cemetery and there were strange symbols on the stone (see fig. 8.1, p. 70).

This grave was for a woman named Bessie Harrell and looked homemade in appearance. It had a banner design on the top with what appears to be, but not for certain due to weathering, the number 333. It also had diamond or rhombus shapes in parts of it, along with arrows and a few dots or tiny holes in places. The word *November* looked interesting as the letter *M* in that word was larger and slanted. Below that was the word *Day,* in which the letters *A* and *Y* seemed to resemble eye glasses looking downward toward the letter *S* in the word *rest*. After looking and wondering if that meant anything at all, I recalled another legend about a Jesse James treasure located very near to this spot. That legend has it that the treasure is in the form of a safe located downstream from an old historic bridge

Fig. 8.1. Gravestone for Bessie Harrell facing east,
unlike others around it.

in Waco that crosses the Brazos River. This legend places the safe
very near the banks of the river, not a mile away from where Dewey
Millay claims it is buried. The letter *M* could represent, according to
some treasure hunters, an owl or Minerva, the Greek goddess of wisdom. The letter *M* is also said to represent the location of a treasure.
In addition, the letter *M* could be read as the number 13 as *M* is the
thirteenth letter of the English alphabet. If that letter *M* is used to
represent the number thirteen, could it represent the thirteen treasures Mr. Millay had mentioned? If that is the case, I thought I may
be on to something.

Looking at the line below that, at the word *Day,* I again noticed the letters *A* and *Y;* the way they were drawn on the headstone looking down like a pair of eyeglasses at the letter *S* in *rest.* I had to wonder then if it was truly a coded message, and if so, what could it be trying to communicate? Of course, I was just playing with this and wasn't certain if it meant anything or not. I was there, and so I took photographs and went home.

Back at home, I got on my computer and pulled up Google Earth just to see how things shaped up, if at all. Now if the letters said anything, I would imagine the *M* could stand for treasure, and if so, the letters *A* and *Y* pointed toward the *S* below. Could it mean if one were to locate the treasure, that they had to look south? Locating that grave on Google Earth, I drew a line due south and it lined up, one mile away, on the banks of the Brazos River, downstream from the old Waco bridge. Right where the other legend said it may be. It couldn't be that simple, could it?

I kept working on this when I had free time, and I tried to locate the landowners of that property as it appeared to be a vacant field. Months went by, and eventually I noticed there was construction on that piece of land, right on the exact location I had been wanting to search. From satellite photos, the construction looked as if it were major, and I wondered who was excavating and what they were doing. It seemed a little more than coincidence that they would dig on the exact spot the map led me to. I had to remind myself that it was probably just a coincidence, and the map was just a hunch. But eventually I found the answer to my question, and it only brings up more questions. That site, where the excavation was taking place, was the site of the new Baylor University football stadium. Coincidence?

Directly across the river from that brand new football stadium is the Texas Ranger Hall of Fame and Museum, which is on the location of the original Fort Fisher. The man who oversaw the building of Fort Fisher was my great-great-great-grandfather, Captain Thomas Hudson Barron.

MODERN REACH OF
AN OLD WEST OUTLAW

The connections listed previously are just the tip of the proverbial ice-berg, as connections with this story have been found linking more modern-day figures with Jesse, other outlaws, and the organizations they had ties to. Figures such as former U.S. President Lyndon Baines Johnson and his alleged "man in the shadows," former Dallas mobster Billie Sol Estes. Another figure who was a friend of President Johnson was Texas State Attorney General Waggoner Carr, who played impor-tant roles in this story along with several other well-known and very powerful figures in the twentieth century. There was also U.S. President Harry S. Truman, who had attended at least one Quantrill Reunion in Missouri—I have a photograph showing my great-great-grandfather, the outlaw Jesse James, sitting on a porch at this same reunion. President Truman's uncle, Jim Chiles, rode with Quantrill and knew Jesse and Frank James well.

Another connection with President Truman takes us back to Jesse James's alias of James L. Courtney. The Courtney family was related in various ways to the James family. The real James L. Courtney's moth-er's maiden name was Andruss. The Andrusses owned a livery stable in Missouri that played an important role in the connection between

THE KANSAS CITY POST, SUNDAY, SEPTEMBER 18, 1921

Fig. 9.1. A Quantrill reunion that President Truman
was said to have attended along with Jesse James
(possibly second from left).

the Courtney and James family showed my late mother. The Andrusses worked in partnership with, first, President Truman's father and, later, Mr. Whitsett, who took over the livery from the Trumans. My mother wrote in her book *Jesse James: The Smoking Gun* that genealogist Laura Anderson Way discovered that the James-Whitsett-Andruss connection proved to be a significant clue in our quest to determine Jesse James's true identity. "[Way's] discovery led to the discovery that President Truman and Jesse James were related through the Woodson line, which in turn explains why Jesse James a.k.a. James L. Courtney had connections to the Whitsett & Andruss Livery, formerly known as Truman & Andruss Livery. Two of the owners, John Truman, father of President Truman, and J. R. Andruss, were his [Jesse James under the alias of James L. Courtney's] cousins."[1]

Fast forward several decades and we find ourselves in Granbury, Texas, at the exhumation of a grave belonging to J. Frank Dalton. At various times in his life, Dalton claimed to be different people. He had claimed to be Billy the Kid and then changed it to Jesse James, to name a few. Stories of Dalton in the treasure hunting world run rampant, mainly because he did have information—credible information—about some of the buried treasures. How did he get that information? It's likely he knew some of the outlaws he claimed to have been, and there are other theories. Regardless of many of the wild claims he made, he was definitely knowledgeable about several large treasure caches. Former attorney general of the state of Texas, Waggoner Carr, was a Jesse James and treasure fan. He knew quite a bit about the treasures, and while he wouldn't say how he knew much of it, he did for a time believe Dalton's claim about being Jesse James. That is, until he met my late mother, Betty Dorsett Duke. After talking with my mother for hours, he changed his mind and was happy to know the truth. In return, he had his driver, Nita Callahan, show us several locations where large treasures had been recovered. We were not disappointed. The first site was located in Georgetown, Texas, approximately two and a half miles west of the Williamson County, Texas, courthouse. It was said to have held a very large cache of gold bars weighing close to eighty pounds each.

Waggoner Carr played a role in the Warren Commission, investigating the assassination of President John F. Kennedy. When interviewed alongside my mother by former news anchorman Bill Kurtis, Mr. Kurtis asked Waggoner Carr about the findings of the Warren Commission, and Waggoner Carr wouldn't say a word. He did give him one of the meanest looks I had ever seen though. It was obvious he didn't like questions dealing with that topic.

The exhumation of Dalton brought out a flood of media from around the country, and we met Waggoner Carr there, too. Another figure present at the exhumation, who Waggoner Carr denied having known, was the notorious Billie Sol Estes, a swindler famous for

Fig. 10.2. Former news anchor and celebrity Bill Kurtis (*left*),
Betty Dorsett Duke, descendant of Jesse James (*center*),
and former attorney general for the state of
Texas Waggoner Carr (*right*).

his wealth, scams, payoffs, cover-ups, and conspiracies implicating the White House.

Another reason for the genealogical information given in chapter 6 is the late Billie Sol Estes. Mr. Estes was well known in the Texas political arena and has been described in varying ways, sometimes as a rascal, a conman, and other times much worse. He was best known for his close association with former U.S. President Lyndon Baines Johnson. After a falling out between the two, Mr. Estes accused President Johnson of various crimes. Billie Sol Estes's family also connects to Clay County, Missouri, as they married into the Courtney, Pence, and Maret families, all of whom were related to Jesse James's family as well as to one another. Billie Sol Estes descended from Abraham Estes and Barbara Brock. (Recall the family tree shown on p. 57.)

After Estes's death in 2013 at age eighty-eight, *The New York Times* printed the following, telling much about his character:

> The rise and fall of Billie Sol Estes was one of the sensations of the postwar era: the saga of a good-ol'-boy con man who created a $150 million empire of real and illusory farming enterprises that capitalized on his contacts in Washington and the gullibility and greed of farmers, banks and agriculture businesses. . . .
>
> As his empire crumbled in 1962, the notoriety of Billie Sol, as nearly everyone in America called him, might have been passing had it not been for the bodies that kept cropping up, for the bribery scandals and fraud in federal farm programs, and for Mr. Estes's own lurid accounts of how it all happened and who was involved.
>
> Many of his statements were self-serving and never proved—particularly allegations about [President] Johnson. Mr. Estes said that he had given millions to Johnson, and that Johnson, while he was vice president, had ordered seven killings disguised as suicides or accidents to cover up his connections to the frauds and had then set up the assassination of Kennedy in 1963 to become president."[2]

While Waggoner Carr and Mr. Estes claimed not to know one another, they had a lengthy conversation, alone, in the corner of the cemetery beneath some shade trees while waiting on the commencement of the exhumation of what was supposed to be J. Frank Dalton's grave. The grave, incidentally, was not the grave of J. Frank Dalton, but was instead that of a member of the Sam Rash family. Nothing came of the exhumation itself, but the goings on around the exhumation were very telling.

Billie Sol Estes had been arrested in frauds that covered the American Southwest and parts of the South. He was alleged to have been involved in agriculture scams dealing with nonexistent grain silos, storage tanks, and many other agriculture- and banking-related crimes. He was said to have bribed agriculture inspectors and anyone else he needed to get what he was after. According to *The New York Times* obituary:

> Soon after the Estes indictments, however, Mr. Freeman, the agriculture secretary, disclosed that a key investigator on the case, Henry Marshall, had been found dead in Texas—bludgeoned on the head, with nearly fatal amounts of carbon monoxide in his bloodstream and five chest wounds from a single-shot bolt-action rifle. Local officials ruled it suicide, but the body was exhumed and the cause changed to homicide.
>
> Six other men tied to the case also died. Three perished in accidents, including a plane crash. Two were found in cars filled with carbon monoxide and were declared suicides. Mr. Estes's accountant was also found dead in a car, with a rubber tube connecting its exhaust to the interior, suggesting suicide, but no poisonous gases were found in the body, and his death was attributed to a heart attack.[3]

In 1963, Mr. Estes was convicted on federal and state charges. In 1984, in a voluntary statement to clear the record, Mr. Estes told a Texas grand jury that Johnson, as vice president in 1961, had ordered that Mr. Marshall, the lead investigator in the case against him, be killed to prevent him from disclosing President Johnson's ties to the Estes conspiracies.[4]

As mentioned in the previous chapters, both President Johnson and Billie Sol Estes were related to the families mentioned in this book through marriage or blood relations. At the beginning of this chapter I mentioned that Billie Sol Estes and Waggoner Carr were both friends of the late president Lyndon B. Johnson. Mr. Estes and Mr. Carr also knew one another; although Waggoner Carr denied that publicly, I personally watched them catching up on old times and laughing with one another in the corner of a cemetery during the exhumation of a grave in Granbury, Texas, in May 2000. Although the exhumation was a bust and the body they were trying to exhume was not that of Dalton, it illustrates two friends of a late president having great interest in Jesse James and at least one of them having great interest in the treasures connected with Jesse. The fact that Estes and President Johnson were distantly related to Jesse suggests that their interest in the treasures and the outlaw may have been passed down through family or other connections that those men may have had.

FURTHERING THE LIGHT
OF FREEDOM AND LIBERTY

In the previous chapter I revealed the names, familial relations, and connections of powerful people along with a few organizations who were involved in the same activities that Jesse and other Old West outlaws were involved in. With the evidence provided, I'm sure most readers would wonder what was going on, and why? I attempt to answer those questions in this chapter.

In my first book, I wrote of the treasures originating in the Middle East and the Temple in Jerusalem. I showed how the treasures moved through history from their original locations, through the Knights Templar, secret societies, and others, through the founding of America, and to the Old West, specifically to Jesse James. Now I will demonstrate how I branched out from Jesse James and his associates and moved forward to our present times. Remember when I mentioned that Jesse, Billy the Kid, and other outlaws of the Old West, as well as powerful political families, colleges, and even the Baptist church all shared a common denominator? On the surface, this common denominator appears to be Freemasonry, but the story goes even deeper than that. There is another player I have yet to discuss, other than a few mentions in my first book, and the addition of this player serves to illustrate to the reader the reason all of this has been going on for centuries and continues even to this day.

Who is this player?

The Catholic Church.

In 1884, Pope Leo XIII wrote in *The Pope and the Freemasons: The Letter "Humanum Genus" of the Pope, Leo XIII, against Free-Masonry and the Spirit of the Age*:

> The race of man, after its miserable fall from God, the Creator and the Giver of heavenly gifts, "through the envy of the devil," separated into two diverse and opposite parts, of which the one steadfastly contends for truth and virtue, the other of those things which are contrary to virtue and to truth. The one is the kingdom of God on earth, namely, the true Church of Jesus Christ; and those who desire from their heart to be united with it, so as to gain salvation, must of necessity serve God and His only-begotten Son with their whole mind and with an entire will. The other is the kingdom of Satan, in whose possession and control are all whosoever follow the fatal example of their leader and of our first parents, those who refuse to obey the divine and eternal law, and who have many aims of their own in contempt of God, and many aims also against God. . . . At every period of time each has been in conflict with the other, with a variety and multiplicity of weapons and of warfare, although not always with equal ardor and assault. At this period, however, the partisans of evil seems to be combining together, and to be struggling with united vehemence, led on or assisted by that strongly organized and widespread association called the Freemasons.[1]

Throughout the centuries the Vatican has, at times, attacked Freemasonry along with many other groups, societies, religions, and beliefs. Several popes throughout history have condemned or proclaimed edicts against Freemasonry and others, with the more dramatic attacks being made public against the Knights Templar on October 13, 1307.

Freemasonry, in my and other researchers' opinions, spawned from the Knights Templar, and it is said the Rosicrucian order did as well. That was likely part of the great allure of Freemasonry for many throughout the centuries, as it offered a place where men could communicate without having to worry about losing their livelihood, the little freedom they had, or even their heads if they said anything the pope didn't agree with. Pope Leo XIII's letter against Freemasonry sounded much like a declaration of war and can be easily read as such. Fortunately, relations have grown much better over the years and calmer dispositions prevail. But that, as is obvious in the letter above, wasn't always the case, and in some cases in the not-too-distant past, the struggle grew violent at times. It boils down to power, I believe. In the case of Pope Leo XIII, I believe he feared a loss of power or the loss of the "hearts and minds" of his congregation. His actions served only to open old wounds and stir discord when, instead, he should have tried sowing the seeds of peace. When you have an organization of any kind, regardless of what the original goal was, men have a tendency to want more, and in wanting more, they step on someone's toes. When that happens, there is conflict, and throughout history we have seen every shade of conflict a person can imagine. The Templar debacle in 1307 was the opening salvo and throughout the years that conflict has waxed and waned—all because others wanted more freedom and liberty.

When a group or a church attacks any other groups or religions or followers of a religion, they leave behind wounds that oftentimes don't heal for years, if not decades, and when those attacks become habitual, the wounds can last for centuries. A perfect example of that is the Vatican's attacks on the Knights Templar followed by their client kingdoms running Jewish people out of various countries. That was followed by the Inquisitions, the brutal attacks on Cathars and other gnostic traditions. These were all based on the judgement of people and nations for simply wanting to practice their beliefs and traditions as they had always done and who, in many cases, tried their best to live peaceably with others.

One good example of this is the infamous pirate Jean Lafitte, who I mentioned in chapter four of this book, when I mentioned that Jesse James and his gang stayed the night at Jean Lafitte's nephew's home while on a robbing spree. In the journal of Jean Lafitte, "he claims to have been born in Bordeaux, France, in 1780 from Sephardic parents whose Conversos grandmother and mother fled Spain for France in 1765, after his maternal grandfather was put to death by the Inquisition for 'Judaizing.'"[2] Freemasons, like so many other groups, were persecuted for religious reasons (or at least, religion was the excuse given for the persecution). Those who had been persecuted, knowing what persecution was like, were likely to have been welcoming to those on the run.

It was from within this context of judgement and religious persecution that families, cultures, religions, Freemasons, and many other groups secured their future. When persecuted, it is all too common for those doing the persecuting to seize the wealth of those they're attacking. Over the years, groups who had become used to being persecuted adapted in that they learned to hide any wealth they may have amassed. In my first book, *Jesse James and the Lost Templar Treasure,* I explained how Jesse James buried his treasures on a grid system, which made the treasure not only easier to locate regardless of whether the topography of the land changed for various reasons, but also because other people were using this grid over the centuries. This grid system predated Jesse and even the founding of the United States of America. I explained how men such as Sir Francis Bacon and his mentor John Dee—in addition to many others throughout history going back through alchemists, Rosicrucians, Jewish rabbis, Sufi mystics, and others to the downfall of the Knights Templar themselves—decided to put their dreams into action and build a nation where people could coexist, enjoy freedom and liberty, and settle their differences in a civilized manner and not have to worry about losing their heads anytime they uttered something that didn't go along with the dogma of the Vatican or the whim of a ruler. I think all of the families listed in this book were involved in building this future, to varying degrees. Some knew much more about what was happening than others, but they all were expected to fulfill certain duties in its creation. Many of them were Freemasons, and while some were not, they still did their part in helping to further the light of freedom and liberty.

These buried treasures weren't about the gold and what the gold could buy. They were about preserving sacred artifacts and other historically significant pieces of information and art. These are things that not only the nation but the world will one day be gifted, when they are ready to receive.

One story of Jesse James's buried treasure comes from a close friend of myself, my family, and, believe it or not, Jesse James: the late George Roming of El Paso, Texas. George was a young boy when he lived just outside of Blevins, Texas, and Jesse was a very old man at that time. It was a few short years before the start of World War II, and Jesse wanted to hire George to help him with an important task. George had to swear an oath of secrecy before Jesse would reveal the secret and the job at hand. George swore his oath and Jesse told him he was going to hire him, that day, to help him move seven hundred bars of gold, weighing approximately fifteen pounds each, to a location within twenty miles of Jesse's home. When they reached that location, George told us that there were two other old gentlemen there, and each of them had hired and sworn a boy about George's age to help bury the gold. They finished burying the gold and returned to their homes. George told us he knew the other two boys never told the secret because they died during the war. George came home from the war, and the older gentlemen he had met and known were also dead. George told us further that he never told a soul that secret until the day he told us. When asked why he told us, George expressed that he felt it belonged to us due to the hard work we put into the research and that we figured out the secret of what happened to Jesse James. He added that we were relatives so he felt we deserved it. Unfortunately, that gold rests on land owned by the U.S. military, and the treasure will be staying there. That said, the knowledge handed down to us from George helped a great deal in the piecing together of these puzzles regarding the treasures and who placed them there. That opened a treasure trove of knowledge for me, which I am sharing with you.

In addition to George telling us that long-held secret, he also mentioned that he was a 32nd degree Scottish Rite Freemason. In talking with him about that, he added that the Catholic Church used to have a secret decree that was active through the 1960s, stating that if a member of the Knights of Columbus could kill a Freemason and get away with it, then they were forgiven of that sin. George was never one to tell stories and was a matter-of-fact sort of man. I believe him and feel that his story illustrates the sense of duty on both sides of that long-hidden war between the Vatican and groups such as the Freemasons, whom the Vatican apparently seemed to fear for some unknown reason.

While that reason may appear to be unknown, it doesn't seem too hard to figure out. The Knights Templar had treasures and the King of France, who was deeply indebted to the Knights Templar along with the Vatican, sought to take that wealth from the Knights Templar, along with any religious artifacts the Knights Templar may or may not have had. The monetary value of the treasure would have given both France and the Vatican a great deal of power. The religious artifacts would have also given them power, as whoever controls the truth controls society. The Vatican and the King of France raided the Knights Templar strongholds and found the coffers had been emptied. They searched for and failed to find that wealth. For years they tortured men like Jaques de Molay in an attempt to find clues to where those treasures may have been taken, but they failed to gain any knowledge. It was obvious that at least a portion of the Knights Templar who escaped had taken those treasures and hidden them. Where?

All of that power was hidden somewhere. I believe that somewhere was the Americas and that it was divided amongst several groups who went about the work of hiding it. Of course, if one group is responsible for hiding it, that means another is actively searching for it. Things like that don't just fade away with the passing of years or even centuries.

Freemasonry and allied groups were said to have been the heirs and caretakers of much of that power. I believe their ultimate goal was and still remains to use that power for the good of the whole and to spread the light of truth for those who seek it. Part of that mission included the formation of the United States of America, modeled after a desire of people around the world to have the freedom and liberties that so many before them had sought, fought for, and died for. In that type of struggle, there are many grey areas, with good men doing bad things for the right reasons or for what at the time seems like their only choice. Families like the James, Estes, Johnson, Lafitte, Baylor, and others mentioned in this book are just a few of those families whose members have played parts in this centuries-long struggle. While various members of those families are seen in positive or negative lights, their actions were no more or less important than those of others and, while important and necessary at the time, pale in comparison to the grand design which amounts to, in my humble opinion, spreading the light of truth, freedom, and liberty to the world. What these families started or carried on will continue to unfold, and their mission will be completed in due time.

Appendix

Connections That Paved the Way

Many have searched for my great-great-grandfather's gold not realizing that priceless treasures were lying within their easy grasp: his personal diaries, written under his alias James Lafayette Courtney. The diaries I've seen include: Volume 1: June 1871 to July 1872 (the original); Volume II: July, 1872 to December, 1872; Volume III: January 1874 to February 1874 and October 1874 to December 1874; and Volume IV: June 1874 to September 1874 and September 1876 to October 1876.

One would naturally assume that if these diaries were really Jesse James's they would be packed full of action. I thought this and was feeling a little let down when I first read them. In fact, I only finished reading them because Jesse, my relative, wrote them. He seemed to have only entered dry, mundane, everyday events and accounts of how much money he made or spent each day. It seemed boring at first, until my eyes finally saw.

Before my great-great-grandfather's diary entries can be linked to Jesse James, one must first be very knowledgeable of the historically accepted version of Jesse James's life and death *and* they must also possess inside information. My great-great-grandfather could have made it easier by simply writing "Jesse James was here," but he instead cached clues to his secret identity in names, places, cipher, and code. The diary entries for his Louisiana trip from January 1–16, 1874, provide a good example because they seemingly have nothing to do with Jesse James, *unless* one is aware that Jesse James is believed to have written them, and that Jesse James is credited with robbing a Louisiana stagecoach on January 8, 1874, and that my great-great-grandfather and Jim Cummins a.k.a. Jim Clark *were on a Louisiana stagecoach* on January 8, 1874, in the very area of the robbery, and that James-Younger Gang member Cole Younger a.k.a. Bud *was in Louisiana* in January 1874. Then the entries becomes very revealing. The more knowledgeable one is about Jesse James, and the more observant one is, the more revealing my great-great-grandfather's diary entries become. He didn't write, "Now watch this, I'm going to switch this guy's real name to his alias and if you're not careful you're going to miss it." It took a third reading of the diary before I ever noticed that Jim Clark became Jim Snodgrass right before my eyes, and there's no telling what I still haven't noticed. The point being that it is almost impossible for anyone to ever discover the hidden messages his diaries hold because only someone who is *really* looking for something would ever notice anything. I guess my great-great-grandfather was feeling pretty cocky that no one would ever figure it out because, though he was operating by now under the alias James L. Courtney, he signed his 1871 diary "J. James" and "JWJ."

In an attempt to correctly identify the individuals my great-great-grandfather mentioned in his diaries, a wide array of genealogical resources was used; however, there is no guarantee that the information presented herein is accurate. Genealogists agree that mistakes are common on census records, and that the information listed on death certificates is only as valid as the informant. In some cases, my great-great-grandfather listed individuals by their given name or surname only, making it almost impossible to positively identify them. However, in the effort to at least *tentatively* identify them, a commonsense approach was used. My claim that Jesse James got away with his own murder has caused quite a controversy among many strictly-by-the-book historians and other self-proclaimed descendants of Jesse James. They claim it is just pure coincidence that some of the names listed in my great-great-grandfather's diaries are identical to the names of known members of the James-Younger Gang. I think they'll have a hard time explaining away so many "coincidences" as they read brief sketches of the individuals listed.

Most members of the James-Younger Gang assumed aliases, and many believe some faked their deaths, just as Jesse James appears to have done. The same goes for some ex-Quantrill men who are not believed to have been members of the James-Younger Gang. Just as historical reports aren't always accurate, neither are old family stories. I like to hear both sides of any story because the truth usually lies somewhere in between. I am hopeful that readers will contact me through my website at jessewjames.wordpress.com with any questions or new information concerning the individuals listed below. There is still much to learn about Jesse James and his gang.

I only included seventy-four of the 321 individuals my great-great-grandfather mentioned in his diaries in this chapter. The names are listed just as my great-great-grandfather wrote them, and like so many of his era, he spelled phonetically. Likewise, I did not correct the spelling of individuals I quoted from various sources. Likewise, I did not correct the spelling of individuals I quoted from various sources though I did silently correct any subtle errors for better readability.

I practically wore out Joanne C. Eakin and Donald R. Hales's *Branded as Rebels: A list of Bushwhackers, Guerrillas, Partisan Rangers, Confederates and Southern Sympathizers from Missouri during the War Years* while researching the following names.[1] Their book is mentioned so often in the list below that I simply refer to it as *Branded as Rebels*.

1. Andruss, Ellen—M. Ellen Andruss was the daughter of Erastus Lafayette 'Rat' Andruss, maternal uncle of the real James L. Courtney.

> Born 1856 Jefferson County, TN, died 1903, Grayson County, Texas. Ellen married Coleman Wilson in 1872 (age 16) Cass County, Missouri, homestead where Denison Dam is now.

It is interesting to note that an edited version of the last will and testament of Charles Younger is included in the Summer 2003 issue of the *James-Younger Gang Journal,* which states that certain "Wilsons were sometimes called by the name of 'Younger' instead of Wilson."*[2] Further, "Charles Younger was the grandfather of Coleman 'Cole,' John, Bob, and Jim Younger."[3]

2. Andruss, Erastus L.—Erastus Lafayette 'Rat' Andruss was the real James L. Courtney's maternal uncle and my great-great-grandfather's friend. My great-great-grandfather listed him as the person to notify in case of his death. Ancestry.com lists the following genealogical information for E. L. Andruss:

> Lafayette Andruss; Alias: 'Rat'; Birth: 17 APR 1824 in Hawkins Co., Tennessee; Death: 28 MAY 1880 in Savoy, Fannin Co., Texas; Census: 1850 Jefferson Co., Tennessee; Occupation: Tinner; Burial: Greenwood Cemetery, Grayson Co., Texas.[4]

Andrews is a variant spelling of Andruss and it appears that E. L. Andruss was often listed as E. L. Andrews. An E. L. Andrews is listed on *The Roster of Confederate Soldiers 1861–1865.* A city directory for Denison, Grayson County, Texas lists E. L. Andruss as E. L. Andruss and E. L. Andrews:

> Andruss, Erastus L, (Andruss & Meyers), Gandy and Armstrong Aves. Andruss & Meyers (Erastus L. Andrews and Peter Meyers),

---

*The Younger's paternal grandfather, Charles Lee Younger, fathered eighteen children by four women. One of these women was his mistress, Parmelia Dorcas Wilson. Charlie Younger died on November 12, 1854. His will stipulated that his eight children by Parmelia were free to change their names from Wilson to Younger. Evidently, when Cole arrived in Corydon he decided that since the Wilsons were using the Younger name, he was free to use theirs.

shoe maker's shop, Main, between Burnet and Fannin Aves. Andruss & Meyers, s s Main [s s could possibly mean shoemaker's shop], between Burnet and Fannin Aves.

According to the Andruss family, E. L. Andruss wouldn't speak to one of his own brothers for years and years because he was a Union soldier. One may find it odd that E. L. Andruss shared a close bond with the real James L. Courtney, who was also a Union soldier. I know I would find it odd if I didn't know that E. L. Andruss wasn't really close to the actual James L. Courtney but instead was close to my great-great-grandfather who assumed the name of James L. Courtney.

Meriam Kokojan, an Andruss family member and genealogist, wrote, "The Civil War was traumatic for the family. On the Union side were Dianna, Orville, George, perhaps Harriet; all in Missouri. On the Confederate side were Dop, Charles, perhaps Erastus, and Margaret—all in Texas. For some twenty years after the War, Orville, in Missouri, was afraid to go visit his brothers in Texas."

Orville's fear of visiting his family in the Sherman/Dennison area of Texas may have been due to the fact that many of Quantrill's men settled in that area after the war, and his brother would have considered him the worst kind of Yankee since he lived in Lawrence, Kansas. In fact, his wife and children were there during the Civil War. Lawrence was the site of Quantrill's infamous raid of August 21, 1863, and was considered the headquarters of the free state of Kansas. Wealthy Jane Andruss lived in Lawrence, Kansas during the Civil War with her oldest four children. George Wesley Andruss was "conscripted to the Confederacy by General Longstreet. Not sympathizing with the Southern cause, George deserted and went to Missouri (where brother Orville and sister Dianna were living) and joined the Union Army. During his enlistment he became acquainted with Hannah Rowland, a schoolteacher, who boarded in Dianna's house."[5] Texas was a Confederate state. E. L. Andruss lived in the Sherman/Denison area, which was the winter headquarters for Quantrill and his men.

The Andruss family claims that James L. Courtney's father, Stephen Courtney, sided with the Union. If true, why would he have been imprisoned in Myrtle Street Prison, St. Louis, Missouri? This prison was for citizens, Confederates, bushwhackers, and guerrillas.[6] He was imprisoned on July 18, 1863, and was released on July 28 of the same year, after he took the "O & B" and posted a $5,000 bond.[7] (O & B refers to the loyalty oath prisoners made to the U.S. government and the bond they posted.)

A letter found in E. L. Andruss's personal wallet indicated that he had connections with Freemasons.[8] It wasn't clear but either James V. Anderson or his father-in-law, Rev. Col. W. M. Dunaway, was the Grand Master, Grand Lodge of Tennessee.[9] Jesse and Frank James are said to have held high positions in the Freemasons.

3. Andruss, H. A.—Harvey "Dop" Adolphus Andruss was born February 18, 1837, in Jefferson County, Tennessee. He was E. L. Andruss's brother (listed above). Dop married Margaret L. Smith on October 8, 1858, at New Market, TN. Within two years they moved to Texas.

Dop served the Confederacy in the same outfit as his brother Charles Andruss down in the Galveston, Texas, area. It is alleged that his wife, Margaret, hated President Lincoln, put down "Negroes," was embittered by the war and afterward felt reduced in circumstances. Dop was always spoken of with love as a kind and gentle man and as a devoted husband and father.

By 1880 Dop lived in Savoy, Texas where his brother Erastus was killed by a tornado. He was listed as a house carpenter and storekeeper in the censuses. By 1900 they had moved to the Bowie, Texas, area by 1900 where Dop ran undertaking and casket making in his basement. Dop died in 1906 in Randlett, Oklahoma, and is buried in the family plot at Bowie, Texas. His wife collected the pension allowed to Confederate veteran's wives.[10]

4. Babe—According to Mae Courtney Thompson, Babe was one of Thomas Barron's black hired hands. Whether or not this was the Babe my great-great-grandfather referred to is not known. A "William N. 'Babe' Hudspeth (Hedgpeth is a variant spelling) was with Quantrill and survived the war. At Pocahontas, Arkansas, five of the guerrillas left Quantrill and turned toward Texas. They were Babe Hudspeth, Rufus Hudspeth, Robert Hudspeth, John Koger, and Oll Shepard. Babe apparently returned to Missouri at a later date because he died May 27, 1907 at St. Joseph Hospital, Kansas City, Missouri."[11]

5. Baby—"Baby" may have been the unidentified Barron my great-great-grandfather referred to as "Barron's Baby." Or "Baby" may have been John Barbee, a fifteen-year-old boy who rode under Quantrill. This could be the Johnson Barbie or Anderson's Baby.[12] The Barron, Courtney, and James families are related to this Barbee family.

6. Barron, Thomas—Lived on Deer Creek (per the diary). Thomas Hudson Barron was my paternal great-great-great-grandfather. He also may have been the father-in-law of Jesse Woodson James. The following article from the *Handbook of Texas,* an online state encyclopedia, gives an overview of his life:

> Thomas Hudson Barron (1796–1874), an early settler and Texas Ranger, son of Susan (Mattingly) and John M. Barron, was born on March 8, 1796, probably in Kentucky. . . . He enlisted in the Kentucky militia at Leitchfield, Kentucky, on November 15, 1814, and participated in the battle of New Orleans on January 8, 1815. He received for his service a bounty grant of 160 acres. By 1817 he was one of the early settlers on the upper Red River in the area of Miller County, Arkansas. He married Elizabeth Carnall in Arkansas on February 20, 1820. In late 1821 Barron, his wife, and first child passed through Nacogdoches with several of the first of Stephen F. Austin's Old Three Hundred colonists. Barron was a

member of the Austin colony for a year before returning to Arkansas Territory. He was commissioned magistrate of Jefferson Township, Miller County, on March 8, 1826. He appears on the tax records for Hempstead County, Arkansas, in 1828, 1829, 1830, and in the census for Hempstead County in 1830.

In January 1831 he returned to Texas, according to Austin's Register of Families. In 1832 he received from Austin a grant of one league of land in Brazos County, located east of Edge on the Old San Antonio Road. During this period Barron contracted to settle at Nashville in Sterling C. Robertson's colony. He was granted twenty-four labors of land now in McLennan County on March 25, 1835, and one labor near the site of present Viesca on June 10, 1835. Throughout his career Barron was active in defense of the frontier. From before until after the Texas Revolution he served as Captain of Texas Rangers at Viesca, Nashville, Washington-on-the Brazos, and Tenoxtitlán, where he was commandant. In January 1836 a ranging company was formed at Viesca with Sterling C. Robertson as Captain and Barron as sergeant. Soon thereafter, Barron was promoted to Captain. As the struggle for Texas independence heightened, Barron, now in middle age, was allowed to return home to assist in moving families and slaves ahead of the advancing Mexican front in the Runaway Scrape. . . .

Early in 1837 Barron's company of rangers established Fort Fisher at Waco Village on the Brazos, at a site within the city limits of present Waco. The reconstructed post is now the site of the headquarters of Company F of the Texas Rangers and the Texas Ranger Hall of Fame and Museum. At Independence, also in 1837, Barron built a house later purchased by Sam Houston. In 1847 Barron homesteaded 320 acres on the Brazos and built the first white homestead on Waco grounds. . . . On April 14, 1851, Barron, as clerk, opened the first district court of McLennan County, with Judge Robert E. B. Baylor presiding. In 1857 or 1858 Barron opened a steam mill on Barron's Branch in Waco, using the bolting system to grind wheat and corn. Machinery for carding wool and cotton was added in 1860. Throughout much of the 1860s Barron served as tax assessor-collector of McLennan County. A street, an elementary school, a creek, and Barron Springs in Waco were named for him.

Barron and his first wife had twelve children, and he and his second wife had ten children. Three of his sons served in the Confederacy during the Civil War. Late in his life he moved to Falls County, near Blevins. He died on February 2, 1874,* at the home of his daughter Mozilla Mixson in Mastersville (now called Bruceville). His remains were moved in December 1976 to First Street Cemetery, Waco, beside the entrance to old Fort Fisher and the Texas Ranger Hall of Fame.

Bill Wilkerson, a known member of the James-Younger Gang, sat up with the family at Barron's death bed, showing that both Wilkerson and Barron had a connection to Jesse.

Thomas Hudson Barron appears to have known my great-great-grandfather before he came to Texas.[13] My great-great-grandfather wrote in his 1871 diary that Barron met him around Stephenville, Texas, as he was making his way to Blevins. and then they rode back to Barron's ranch together. (My great-great-grandfather is believed to have referred to Thomas Hudson Barron by the following names: "Pa, Paw, the old man, the old gentleman, and the Captain.")[14]

I later found information that may explain how Barron and my great-great-grandfather knew each other before their meeting near Stephenville: "Captain Barron lived in Arkansas as a pioneer with J. G. W. Pierson, Walter F. Pool and others who came to Texas before

---

*Theron Palmer, author of the above article, indicated a different date of death for Thomas Hudson Barron than my great-great-grandfather recorded in his diary, where he wrote on February 24, 1874: "Tusday at thads me & all the family & Pa died this morning at six o'cl[ock] & we sent for the to [illegible] and they shaved him & ma & them dressed him he had the best coat and pants that could be had anywhere & we sent an got the coffin"

1830."[15] The following quote further explains: "After the death of his wife Purity, J. G. W. Pierson left Kentucky with some of his friends and relatives including his three children and son-in-law, Jonathan Pool, and headed westward. He settled at Pecan Point, then Miller County, Arkansas, now Red River County, Texas, where he became acquainted with and married in late 1826 to Elizabeth Montgomery, the daughter of William Montgomery and (Mary) 'Polly' James, an aunt of Frank and Jesse James. [Mary 'Polly' James was the daughter of Jesse and Feby James.]"[16] From all indications Thomas H. Barron was very well acquainted with Jesse James's family.

The following quote indicates there are even more connections between the Barron family and Jesse James: "My grandmother, Minnie Crabtree Barron, used to tell me stories about her father, my great-grandfather, riding with the James Gang. My grandfather was Randolph Barron, born in 1874 and died in 1948. I don't know my great-great-grandfather's first name or any info about him."[17] *The Waco Tribune Herald* reported "The City of Waco requested permission to exhume the remains of Thomas Hudson Barron in July of 1976 as their Bi-Centennial project. Descendants of Thomas Hudson Barron were contacted and no one objected." According to the application for the court's permission, "The commission desires to honor Capt. Barron by reentering his remains at a location that has been dedicated as memorial to the Texas Rangers and the important role that the Rangers played in the early development and growth of Texas."[18]

7. Barron, Travis—Son of Thomas Hudson Barron and his first wife, Elizabeth Carnall.

> Birth: 3 NOV 1839 in Washington Co., Texas; Death: 15 NOV 1891 in McLennan Co., Texas; Census: 1850 Milam Co., Texas; Event: Census # 2 1870 McLennan Co., Texas; Occupation: Farmer; Military Service: 13 APR 1861 2nd Texas Cavalry (CSA), enlisted at Weatherford, Texas; Event: Census # 3 1880 McLennan Co., Texas.

Marriage 1 Elizabeth J. Mixon b: 21 JUN 1844 in Texas; Married: 13 JAN 1866 in McLennan Co., Texas.

Travis had a twin brother named Milam, but it has not yet been determined whether they were identical or fraternal twins. Travis enlisted 2 Apr 1862 at Waco in 19th TX Cav (Buford's Reg) under Capt. Stone. Milam Barron's CSA enlistment document describes him as being twenty-two years old, 5'11" tall with black hair and hazel eyes.[19]

Another source states about Travis's brother that "Milam died in the Civil War while serving in the Confederate States Army—married Miss S. A. Lott, but had no issue (children)."[20]

8. Blackwell, J.—May have been the James "Jim" Blackwell who rode with the James-Younger Gang.

The following Blackwells were veterans who enlisted in Falls County, lived or were buried there post-Civil War, or belonged to the Falls County Willis L. Lang Camp of Confederate Veterans:

Blackwell, John T., b. 24 Apr 1837, d. 5 Apr 1911, Bur. Clover Hill Cem, Co A, 11 AL Inf
Blackwell, W. J., b. -, d. -, bur. -, Co K, Hardy's AR Inf.[21]

The *Daily Democrat* of Marlin, Texas, printed on July 12, 1907: "W. J. Blackwell, an aged citizen of the Durango community, died at his home on Deer Creek Thursday night. He had resided in that section for many years and was highly respected by all who know him. He was a Mason, being a member of Durango Lodge. Was a Confederate soldier, having enlisted in Company K, Hardy's brigade of infantry in Arkansas. He leaves a number of relatives at Durango. The remains will be interred in the Cego cemetery with Masonic honors."[22]

Information linking Blackwells to Jesse James:

- "... James 'Jim' Blackwell supposedly rode or associated with Jesse James (James Gang). Mr. Blackwell was shot in Little Rock, AR, [Year unknown] and died at a local hospital when the doctors were trying to remove the bullet."[23]
- A "J. Blackwell" was in the 5th Missouri Cavalry associated with General Joe Shelby who was closely connected to Frank and Jesse James: "This unit was attached to Cols. Joseph G. Shelby's (wounded 4 July 1863) & G. W. Thompson's 1st Brigade of Brig. Gen. John S. Marmaduke's Division, Lt. Gen. Theophilus H. Holmes' District of Arkansas in Lt. Gen. Edmund Kirby Smith's Trans-Mississippi Department and was commanded by Lt. Col. B.F. Gordon."[24]
- "J. Blackwell" was in the 5th Missouri Cavalry: "Name: J. Blackwell; Company: I; Unit: 5 Missouri Cavalry; Rank[at] Induction: Private; Rank[at] Discharge: Private; Allegiance: Confederate;"[25] and
- "I am interested in the Blackwells who went from Alabama to Texas. My ggrandmother Nancy Ann Blackwell m Josiah Durden in 1832, in Autauga County Alabama. After the Civil War there was a Blackwell 'gang' in Chilton County, Al (Chilton was cut from Autauga) who were killing Yankees and Yankee sympathizers. The Blackwell brothers were ambushed and escaped to Texas."[26]

9. Bolton—Bolton was a photographer in Waco, Texas, who took four photos each of my great-great-grandfather, Mary Ellen (his wife), and their first child, Anah, on October 2, 1872. Bolton may have been:

Thomas Bolton; Age in 1870: 36; Estimated Birth Year: 1833; Birthplace: Missouri; Home in 1870: Waco, McLennan, Texas; Race: White; Gender: Male; Post Office: Waco; Roll: M593_1598; Page: 41; Image: 78; Year: 1870[27]

It is interesting to note that Martha Bolton was the sister of Charley and Bob Ford, the men who allegedly killed Jesse James.

10. Bonner—A possible Jesse James connection. N. S. Bonner was a Master Mason in the same Masonic Lodge my great-great-grandfather belonged to in 1873.[28]

Newton Bonner, born in Tennessee, lived at age twenty-six in the household of Thomas Bonner in 1870. Thomas Bonner was fifty-six in 1870 and was born in North Carolina.[29] Falls County, Texas, Civil War records list the following:

Newton S. Bonner was born in 1846, d. -, bur. - , Co H, 11 TN Cav.[30]

An interesting post concerning Z. D. Bonner and the James-Younger Gang connects to the Falls County Bonners: "Yes, I know Zaron Deloss Bonner! He was my great-great-grandfather and he was a blacksmith in Kansas in 1872. He had at least one shop in a community called Cato. I believe it was in Crawford County, close to Pittsburg, KS. Our oral history says he shoed horses for the Jesse James Gang, but no proof."[31] Z. D. Bonner's blacksmith shop was located in the southeast corner of Kansas within fifty miles of the Oklahoma border and about five miles west of the Missouri border, which means it was on what is referred to as the Texas Trail, the road most commonly used for traveling from Missouri to the Dennison/Sherman area of Texas. Quantrill and his men, including Frank and Jesse James, are known to have traveled that route frequently. "The James-Younger Gang traveled to and from Texas and Missouri through Indian Territory on the Texas Trail, now Eastern Oklahoma, down through Miami, Venita, Adair, Pryor, Tullahassee, Muskogee, Stringtown, Atoka, Caddo, Durant, and Colbert to Denison, Texas. The Texas Trail was a commonly used road by outlaws and common people alike. The Butterfield Stage route that ran from Ft. Smith, Arkansas to Denison, Texas was just east of the Texas Trail."[32]

It is intriguing that the aforementioned Z. D. Bonner shod horses for the James-Younger Gang and his brother, C. C. Bonner, lived in Falls County, Texas (where my great-great-grandfather lived): "Christopher Columbus Bonner is the brother of my great-great-grandfather, Zora D. Bonner. They are two of 14 children of Thomas and Elizabeth Dodson Bonner. C. C. was born February 14, 1840 in Warren County Tennessee and died April 29, 1914 and is buried in Mart, Texas. He married Ellen Elizabeth Wright on September 28, 1870 in Falls County, Texas."[33] C. C. Bonner served the Confederacy:

> Bonner, C. C., b. 14 Feb 1840, d. 29 Apr 1914, bur. Mart, TX, Lt, Co G, 35 TN Inf, Cleburn's Brig.[34]

Jimmy "Mantooth" Kimmey told me that he is related to the Dorsetts (my mother's maiden name) and the Bonners, and Mantooth has always heard that some of the Bonners rode with the James-Younger Gang. He also heard that some of the James-Younger Gang's stolen loot helped purchase the Bonner Plantation in East Texas.

11. Brewer—*Branded as Rebels* lists a "_____ Brewer as a Guerrilla."[35]

The following Brewers lived in the same precinct in Falls County, Texas, that my great-great-grandfather did:

> Brewer, S. B., age forty-seven, white male, born in Mississippi; J. O. Brewer, age thirty-eight, white male, born in Georgia; Brewer, F. B., age twenty-five, white male, born in Arkansas.[36]

Oliver P. "Ollie" Roberts a.k.a. "Brushy Bill" Roberts of Hico, Texas, claimed to be the infamous Billy the Kid and mentioned riding with a Brewer and a Widenmann (who is also listed in my great-great-grandfather's diary).[37] Jesse James and Billy the Kid reportedly knew each other.[38]

Bob Brewer, a professional treasure hunter and coauthor of

The Shadow of the Sentinel, now entitled *Rebel Gold,* substantiates the above story with the following information (written verbatim):

> My GGrandpa on Mom's side was Stonewall Jackson Mathes, Mathews, Matthews. He used all three spellings at different times in his life. He also used the initials J. C. and C. We have no idea why he used so many names but Mom always said he knew and rode with outlaws. He did know Billy the Kid if you can believe the story. I do.
>
> J. C. and his wife ran a boarding house out in far west Texas near the NM line. Billy the Kid would stay there once in a while. Family oral history says, Billy loved kids and used to hold and rock my Grandmother and her sister when he was around. Of course lots of stories like this so who really knows. J. C. was a lawman off and on as were many of the outlaws. He said he was a Texas Ranger too, and I have a cousin who said he used to have a photo of a ranger troop with him in it. The picture went to some of the other kin when he died.[39]

12. Broomfield, Jo—May have been Josie Broomfield, born in Texas, a twenty-two-year-old white female living in Falls County, Texas, in 1880.[40]

Ben Broomfield rode with Quantrill and was in the Lawrence Raid. Depending on which report one reads some have him being killed on several different dates during the Civil War, and some claim that he rode with Jesse James after the war.[41] For example, "One night in July, during the summer of 1864, Jesse James, Arch Clements, Ben Broomfield, Jim Anderson, and Luke Bissell went to the house of Harry Tumy, a Union man."[42]

13. Broomfield, Wood—Brumfield is a variant spelling for Broomfield. This man may have been the Woodson S. Broomfield with Poindexter and Jesse James.

Woodson S. Broomfield was with J. A. Poindexter.*[43] He is said to have died of disease while a POW at Alton, Illinois on November 21, 1862.[44] I don't think he did, just as Joe Poindexter and others may not have died as reported.† He appears to have joined the many other former members of Quantrill's guerrillas who went to Texas.

After checking all census records available to me ranging from 1790–1930 using Heritage Quest Online, I found only two Woodson Broomfields/Brumfields and only one Woodson S. Brumfield:

Broomfield, Woodson, Age 60, Male, White, Born in Kentucky but living in Hartford, Ohio in 1870—also listed as Brumfield in the 1860 census records in Hartford, Ohio.

The other Broomfield was listed as

Brumfield, Woodson, Single, Age 36, Male, White, Born in Kentucky and living in Columbia, Boone County Missouri in 1860.

It stands to reason that the Woodson S. Brumfield/Broomfield from Missouri was the one who rode with Quantrill's guerrillas, and was probably the Wood Broomfield my great-great-grandfather mentioned in his diary. Wood Broomfield also served in the regular Confederate Army:

---

*From the Ancestry.com Civil War Service Records: "J. A. Poindexter—A Colonel, who was with Colonel Porter, began guerrilla warfare in Missouri by assembling small bands on July 20, 1862. He was commissioned by General Sterling Price to recruit for the Confederate Army. He made a raid into Livingston County in 1862. He also skirmished with Federal troops in Carrol County in July 1862. He died at his residence in Randolph County, Missouri, on April 14, 1869. Ref: NW Missouri, 1915; Castel; Bartels; O.R.; Liberty Tribune, April 30, 1869; Randolph, 1884."

†Eakin and Hale state in *Branded as Rebels:* "He (Woodson Broomfield) was arrested along with Henry Hill and charged with the murder of the Union man, McClatchey. He lived near Bluffton, Missouri. He did not die in prison." They also state about Henry Hill: "with his son-in-law, [was] living near Bluffton, Missouri. Both were arrested and charged with the murder of a Union man named McClatchey who was killed in October 1861. They were taken to Mexico, Missouri and tried by a military commission."

Surname: Broomfield; Given Name: Woodson; Middle Initial: S; Company: F; Unit: Rank - Poindexter's Reg't, Missouri Cav.; Induction Rank: Private; Discharge: Private; Allegiance: Confederate.[45]

The following post from the Broomfield Family Forum on the internet claims that a Broomfield rode with Jesse James, and that some Broomfields were known as Martins (written verbatim):

Frances Broomfield b1819 in ky. Married a martin, had 3 kids:. william "dommie" broomfield..nancy broomfield and then 3 step kids that apparently assumed the broomfield name after their mother's death. one census shows them as martins and then a few years later after they moved to Mo with frances. show them as broomfields. they are susan martin affiah martin and john martin. samual k broomfield born to henderson broomfield had a brother ben broomfield who rode with jesse james. they are from gable co mo. samual was from cooper co. moved to Clay Co (MO) after the civil war. william "dommie" broomfield.is my great great grandfather. he married martha ann carroll (childhood friend of jesse james).[46]

The following information shows the discrepancies in dates and places of Ben Broomfield's historically reported death (written verbatim):

Benjamin Broomfield served under Quantrill. Benjamin was part white and part Comanche. In the 1860 Missouri census, Jackson County, Westport, the Broomfields lived with Malinda Fitzwater. Benjamin was born in Missouri and married a Miss Jordan some-time in 1864. [A Jordan is also listed in my great-great-grandfather's diaries.]

On August 13, 1863 at Flat Rock Ford over the Grand River,

Broomfield pulled Peyton Long up behind him to safety. Their horse was shot out from under them. Broomfield also took part in the Lawrence Massacre, and fought in the Boonville skirmish on September 15, 1864. He fought Johnson at Centralia and left with the rear guard. After Centralia Broomfield took the wounded Plunk Murray to safety, but Federal troops were too close behind them, so he and William Stuart turned and attacked the troops in order to let Murray and Ling Litten get away. He was killed in the attempt. Another source claims Broomfield was killed in 1863, but Hamp Watts thought he was killed near Booneville around September 20, 1864.[47]

The 1880 census for Falls County, Texas, shows that an F. M. Broomfield, age twenty-five, white male, lived in the 7-PCT. Ben lived next to Frank E. Krause, the grandfather of Bonnie Parker, of Bonnie and Clyde fame. Frank Krause lived on the farm next to my great-great-grandfather's farm.[48]

14. Burnett—Connected to the Youngers, Quantrill, and Bob Ford.

My great-great-grandfather made the following diary entry on July 1, 1871: "Saturday morning in camp at Burnett's on Denton Creek and then started for Elizabethtown and crossed Denton 2 mile from camp. . . ."

The fact that the Burnett my great-great-grandfather referred to was living on Denton Creek in Texas indicates that he was some of Jeremiah Amos Burnett's family. He also mentioned being in Elizabethtown, where many other Burnetts lived. Jeremiah was the father of Samuel Burk Burnett, founder of the famous Four Sixes Ranch. My great-great-grandfather also mentioned M. Crowley in his diary, which is interesting because there is a Crowley connection to Jeremiah Burnett's family.

A number of Burnetts from Missouri lived in or near Denton County, Texas, in 1870, and they are probably all of the same family:

Burks Burnett, age twenty-one, white male, Elizabethtown, Denton County, Texas, which is located near Denton, Texas; James Burnett, age twenty-seven, white male, Elizabethtown, Denton County, Texas; Jerry Burnett, age forty-seven, white male, Elizabethtown, Denton County, Texas; Reuben Burnett, age thirty-five, white male, Elizabethtown, Denton County, Texas; and Samuel H. Burnett, age forty-three, white male, Elizabethtown, Denton County, Texas.[49]

The following is also available about Samuel Burnett:

Samuel H. Burnett: Birth: 1826 in Dist. 6, Bates Co., MO; Burial: Family Cem., Temple, OK.[50]

Burnett, Samuel, 22, farmer . . . MO, Elizabeth, 17, MO.[51]

Samuel H. Burnett, not having a family of his own, left the Burnett Ranch in Texas and joined the Confederate Army and was commissioned a captain. Because he had ties in Missouri, a northern state, the Confederacy asked him to return to Missouri and work as what they called then, a "double agent." So Sam rode to Missouri and joined the Union Army as a private. He served the entire war in the Union Army as a private, but a spy for the Confederacy. At the end of the war, rather than letting the news be known that he was really a Confederate captain, Sam Burnett accepted his discharge papers at Benton Barracks in St. Louis and rode home to Texas.[52]

Rootsweb gives the following:

Burnett, Saml, 43, farmer . . . MO
Ann E., 32, MO
Reuben, 11, works on farm, MO
Lee, 5, MO

Marion, m, 3, TX

Father: Samuel Sr. BURNETT b: 1791 in Montgomery or Patrick Co., VA

Mother: Levenia "Leah" COX b: 1793 in Patrick Co., VA

Marriage 1 Mrs. Samuel II (Ann Elizabeth) BURNETT b: 1833 in MO

Married: ABT 1849 in Bates Co., MO

    Children: 1. Reuben BURNETT b: 1859 in Bates Co., MO

2. Lee BURNETT b: 1865 in Bates Co., MO

3. Marion BURNETT b: 1867 in Denton Co., TX[53]

Samuel's obituary was in the *Fort Worth Star-Telegram*, June 29, 1922:

S. B. Burnett, 74, Texas pioneer cowman, died Tuesday. He had been ill for a number of years, but seemed much better at Christmas, spending some time in Mineral Wells, but sustained a second stroke on Christmas Day. Funeral services will be held Wednesday afternoon, with burial in East Oakwood Cemetery. Rev. L. D. Anderson, pastor of the First Christian Church, of which Captain Burnett was a member, will officiate. Early Tuesday morning men who had helped Burnett in his many endeavors began passing before his bier in a steady stream and telegrams of condolence have been received from all parts of the state.

Samuel Burk Burnett was born in Bates County, Mo. Jan. 1, 1849, son of Jeremiah Burnett and Nancy Turner. In the late 1850s the jayhawkers and ruffians of the Kansas border became a great menace to life and property. After his home was burned, Jerry Burnett sold what he had left and emigrated southward. He had intended stopping in the area which later became the Indian Territory, but decided to continue his journey, settling on Denton Creek, within 45 or 50 miles of Fort Worth. Samuel Burk Burnett spent his early life on the frontier and at age 16, went to school for two or three years at a little place now called Prairie Point. He met W. T. Waggoner* there and the two formed a friendship that lasted for half a century.

When Burk Burnett left school, he returned home and took up management of his father's ranch. In 1871, he took a herd of about 1200 cattle to Abilene, Kansas, heading the outfit of eight or ten men, the youngest man in charge of a herd on the Chisholm Trail at the time. The same year he married Ruth Loyd, daughter of M. B. Loyd, late president of the First National Bank of Fort Worth. Three children were born to them: Thomas L., (half owner of the ranch at Burk Station); Frances, (died age 18 months) and Annie (married Charles A. Johnson of Denver and died a few years ago).

In 1873, Burnett started to Kansas with another herd in which he had half interest. He used his "6666" brand on these cattle—it later became one of the most famous in Texas. The profit from this sale was the real beginning of the young cattleman's fortune. In the following years he made a study of the cattle business and did as much as any one man to make it a science. He was a pioneer in the work of grading the native Texas long-horned steer and was perhaps the first man to adopt the plan of buying steers and holding them for the market—a plan so good that other ranchmen soon followed.

After family trouble caused a separation and divorce from his wife, Burnett and his father-in-law dissolved partnership in the cattle business, but still held jointly the land at Burk Station, comprising the "6666" Ranch. They continued to be friends until Loyd's death some years later.

When the time came to give up his Indian land pastures, Burnett managed to obtain a stay of several months (thus avoiding a heavy monetary loss) by obtaining the intercession of President Theodore Roosevelt. This was the beginning of a lasting friendship with the

---

*W. T. Waggoner was the son of Dan Waggoner, founder of the famous Waggoner Ranch. My great-great-grandfather also mentioned Dan Waggoner in his diary; see page 74 of this book for more on Waggoner.

"Rough Rider" and afterward, Burnett was host to the President when he took his famous wolf hunt in Texas.

In 1892, Burnett married the widow of Dr. Claude Barradal, a daughter of J. R. Couts of Weatherford. A son of this union, Burk Jr., died in 1916 just before reaching maturity. His death was a hard blow for the young man was the idol of his father who had planned great things for this son of his old age.

In 1904, Burnett bought what was known as the "8 Ranch" in King County comprising 141,000 acres and 15,000 head of stock. He then began to buy up bordering lands in that county and has more than 200,000 acres under fence. The name was later changed to "6666" Ranch [the famous Four Sixes].

About five years ago, Burnett donated to the City of Fort Worth the tract of land at Seventh and Lamar Streets known as Burk Burnett Park, razing several structures to clear it for park purposes.

At the time of his death, Burnett was considered one of the wealthiest men in the southwest, owning more than 260,000 acres of land, several thousand head of cattle, the Burk Burnett office building in Fort Worth, bank stock in several cities, in addition to personal and real holdings. Oil strikes further increased his wealth.

Immediate survivors of Captain Burnett are son, Tom Burnett of Wichita Falls; granddaughter, Miss Anne Burnett of Fort Worth; two sisters, Mrs. J. M. Barkley and Mrs. John Roberts of Wichita Falls and brother, T. G. Burnett of Benjamin, as well as several nieces and nephews.

Quoting a friend associated with the National Stockyards in Illinois, "Fort Worth and the State of Texas has lost a good and worthy man. To have enjoyed the friendship of Capt. Burnett I hold one of the greatest privileges of my life."

The *Oklahoma City Oil Journal,* March 14, 1931, reported the following information regarding Bob Ford's assassin and his connection with the Burnetts. (Recall that Bob Ford was the alleged assassin of Jesse James.)

> Both Roe and Joe Burnett were among the city's early day officers, the family being pioneers who helped blaze the trail of civilization in the southwest. The family is related to the late Captain S. Burk Burnett, famous pioneer of Texas, who owned the Burkburnett Ranch. The late Joe Burnett, uncle of Sam Burnett, engaged in a hand-to-hand struggle with "Red" Kelley, a noted outlaw, a number of years ago. Burnett had arrested Kelley near the old Frisco depot. During the struggle Burnett killed the outlaw. Kelley was the slayer of Bob Ford, outlaw and former partner of Jesse James.

The following post mentions the Younger and Quantrill connection to Samuel Burk Burnett's family:

> I am a descendant of George Burnet and Margaret Cunningham, who came to Pittsylvania County, VA sometime between 1740 and 1755. They had a son named James Burnet (1720/35–1797), who had a large family. His son, James Cunningham Burnett (1776–1839) was my ancestor, and this particular group of Burnetts includes the lineage of Peter Hardeman Burnett, the first governor of California. Every family has its 'dark' side, and this particular line also was related to the Youngers, outlaws who were associated with the Dalton gang and the James brothers. Cole Younger, the most notorious of the Youngers, rode with William Quantrill and participated in the raid on Lawrence, Kansas in 1863.[54]

15. Cage—Lives in Stephenville, Texas; possibly connected to the Youngers.

The 1910 Federal Census records for Stephenville, Erath County, Texas, show that James H. Cage was sixty-four in 1910 and was born about 1846 in Texas.[55] The tombstone marking his grave in West End Cemetery (section seven) indicates that he was born in 1845 and died in 1912; Janie, wife of J. H. Cage, was born in 1855 and died in 1937.[56] Another source tells us "James H. Cage lived in Stephenville, Texas (Erath County). . . .There is a James H. Cage, sixteen years old, a clerk, listed on the 1860 federal census records living in a hotel or boarding house owned by a merchant named Toliver in Erath County, Texas. James H. Cage's father died in the 1850s and his mother married a Mr. Toliver. J. H. Cage married Miss Jane Boykin."[57] The Cage listed in our great-great-grandfather's diaries may be connected to the Youngers. It is alleged that the Youngers and James were related. The following posting on the internet's Cage Family Forum tells about the Younger/Cage connection: "After being left a widow by the Civil War, my ggg grandmother, Mary Bomar Younger gave her youngest children to a trader, a Mr. Cage, who took them into TN. He kept one and changed his name to CAGE."[58]

An online contributor adds: "Mr. Cage's name was MILTON CAGE, and Mary Bomar in a deed said that he was the father of John Henry Wilson Younger: Mary ('Polly') Bomar (Younger): I, Polly Younger, Halifax County, in consideration of the natural love and affection I have for my son, John Henry Wilson Younger. . . . The condition of the above obligation is that if the above John Henry Wilson should die without heirs, then the same property shall go to my friend, Milton Cage, the father of the above John Henry Wilson Younger."[59]

Another website stated "John Henry Wilson Younger was born about 1818 in Halifax, Virginia. His parents were Williamson Younger, born about 1796, Halifax, Virginia, and Mary Bomar, born about 1798, Halifax, Virginia. James Younger, born: ABT 1810 – Halifax, Virginia; John Younger Born: ABT 1814 – Halifax, Virginia; Armistead Younger Born: 1811 – Halifax, Virginia; Williamson Younger Born: JAN 1817 – Halifax, Virginia."[60]

Census records show "James H. Cage, sixteen years of age, a clerk, listed on the federal census records living in a hotel or boarding house owned by a merchant named Toliver in Erath County, Texas. On August 11, 1860 he is listed on the Slave Schedule for Erath County as owning three slaves: one black male sixty years old; and two black females, one fifty years old and the other seventeen years old."[61]

It is interesting that J. H. Cage's funeral records showed that he named a son "John 'Migonega' Cage allegedly after a tavern keeper by the name of John Migonegal, age 35, from PA, listed in the 1860 federal census records as living in the same hotel ran by Mr. Toliver (J. H. Cage's mother married a Mr. Toliver.)"[62]

16. Caldwell—A possible Quantrill connection. The following James Caldwell may have been the Caldwell my great-great-grandfather referred to:

James Caldwell; Age in 1870: 35; Estimated Birth Year: 1834; Birthplace: Alabama; Home in 1870: Precinct 1, Falls, Texas; Race: White; Post Office: Marlin; Roll: M593_1584; Page: 7; Image: 13; Year: 1870.[63]

A "Jim Caldwell rode with Quantrill and is said to be buried in an unmarked grave in Pleasant Hill Cemetery [Missouri, I presume]."[64] A James Caldwell is listed among the bushwhackers, guerrillas, Partisan Rangers, Confederates, and Southern sympathizers from Missouri during the War Years: "James Caldwell was with Snider's Missouri Cavalry Killed by Missouri State Militia while he was a POW in Lewis County, Missouri on October 13, 1862. Ref: CSRJC. A _____ Caldwell was with Porter. Ref: Block."[65]

17. Campbell—May have been the man described as "Uncle Charlie Campbell died Apr 12, 1907 at the age of 107 yrs 1 mo & 28 days; Veteran of Black Hawk Indian, Texas Independence & Mexican Wars," buried in Blevins Cemetery, Falls County, Texas.[66]

Other Campbells resided in Falls County, Texas, in 1870 including Charles, John, and George.[67] Or the Campbell my great-great-grandfather referred to may have been the Campbell mentioned in connection with other Quantrill men: "On August 20, 1864 he was with Thrailkill, Yeager, Todd, Taylor, and Thornton. Taylor lost his arm August 18 (19), 1864, at Lafayette. Campbell may have been with him at this time."[68] Andrew Anderson Campbell[69] and Doc Campbell[70] rode with Quantrill.

18. Cary, D.—A Daniel Carey is listed in *Branded as Rebels* as a "rejected or challenged voter in the Platte County elections of 1866 (due to Southern sympathies)."[71]

One source indicates that the Daniel Carey in Falls County, Texas, in 1870 was a native Texan. In 1870 he was twenty-six and married to a woman named Texana;[72] however, another source alleges that Daniel Carey was born in Indiana:

Daniel Joel Carey; Birth: 26 Feb 1845 in West Braden, Orange County, Indiana; Death: 12 Apr 1921 in Waco, McLennan County, Texas; Burial: Apr 1921 Old First Street Cemetery, Waco, McLennan County, Texas; Census: 1850 North West Township, Orange County, Indiana; Census: 1870 Falls County, Texas; Census: 1880 Falls County, Texas; Census:1920 Waco, McLennan County, Texas. Marriage 1 Texana 'Annie' Foster b: Mar 1851 in Sabine Town, Sabine County, Texas on 7 Sep 1870 in Robertson County, Texas.[73]

19. Cates, Robert at Decatur, Texas—Connected to the James-Younger Gang as well as the Dalton Gang.

Some members of the Cates family were in Missouri before coming to Texas.[74]

The parents of Robert Granville Cates Sr. were Charles D. Cates Sr. & Narcissa M. McMillen. Charles D. Cates died in Bradley

County, TN circa 1847 and Narcissa McMillan Cates having gone with the children to Texas died on 16 Jul 1892 in Wise County, TX and is buried in Sand Hill Cemetery there. Robert Granville Cates siblings were Montaville Cates; Mary Cates; David C. Cates; Elizabeth J. Cates who married Posey P. R. Collom; Joseph R. Cates; Charles Donoho Cates; and Dewitt Claiborne Cates.[75]

Robert Cates served the Confederacy:

Co. B; 15 Texas Cavalry. Rank Induction: Private; Rank Discharge: Private; Allegiance: Confederate.[76]

And according to another source, "Robert Cates lived in Decatur, Wise County, Texas; Township: Decatur Precinct 3."[77] Robert Cates was the Sheriff of Wise County, Texas from August 6, 1860 to August 1, 1864.

Robert Cates August 6, 1860, to August 1, 1864; December 2, 1873, to February 15, 1876. Robert Cates was born on January 8, 1836, in McMinn County Tennessee. Due to the death of his father, Charles Cates, the family migrated west to Collin County, Texas, in the fall of 1854. That next year, 1855, Robert Cates advanced even further west, settling in Wise County. The spring of that year he married Elizabeth Taylor, daughter of Judge Frank Taylor, an early chief justice. They had ten children and in 1907, his third son, William Cates, became the first elected sheriff of Stephens County, Oklahoma.

On August 6, 1860, he was elected to his first term of office and served until August 1, 1864. He served throughout the Civil War. Robert Cates was a part of two different demonstrations that occurred in Wise County. The first being the Peace Party conspiracy which occurred in the summer of 1862. The Peace Party was an organization of men who were Union sympathizers and others having no loyalty to either the North or the South. One group was in Cooke County the other was in Prairie Point, now known as Rhome, their objective was to take over the Confederate forces stationed in this area, but the Confederate forces got wind of what was being planned. The Peace Party conspiracy concluded with five men being hung in a clearing west of Decatur and the ropes were tied by Cates.*

The second demonstration was by the Union League. The Union League had grievances against Robert Cates and his brother, Charles. The Union League members were upset with Robert Cates because of his involvement in the Peace Party trails. "He was unable to obtain very little education, but his sharp conflicts with nature and men have developed him into a man of unusual shrewdness and strength of intellect. In his early scouting about the county as sheriff he dared the Indians, and defied the elements, and grew to be a stalwart defender of the county and prosecutor of criminals."

On one confrontation with the Indians, Cates had received information about some cattle rustling in the southern part of the county. Cates mounted his horse and went to investigate. When he arrived in the area, he located the subjects. The Indians attacked and Cates was injured. An arrow had pierced his leg and pinned him to the

---

*The Texas State Historical Association Handbook of Texas online explains that "In 1862 Wise County was gripped by the same Union League conspiracy hysteria that precipitated the Great Hanging at Gainesville. Five men were tried and hung for plotting to aid the Union cause by burning property, stealing weapons, and reducing 'the people to helplessness.' When the war ended, an angry mob of 200 people protested the hangings but was dispersed by local supporters of law and order. Though many Wise County inhabitants remained bitter in defeat, the Reconstruction county governments usually included both ex-Confederates and Republican party appointees. Indian raids continued until 1875, and the population of the county grew slowly. Only 1,450 people resided in Wise County in 1870. During the antebellum period Decatur was a stop on the Butterfield Overland Mail route from St. Louis, Missouri, to San Francisco, California. A government telegraph line also connected the county with larger population centers. Between 1866 and 1886 the Eastern Cattle Trail to Abilene, Kansas, crossed Wise County east of Decatur. The coming of the railroads eventually provided a more convenient and cheaper means of transportation for crops and livestock."

cantle on his saddle. Luckily Cates' horse was fresh and he was able to out run the Indians. When he arrived back in Decatur, the local physician had to remove Cates from his horse, saddle and all.[78]

Joseph R. Cates, brother of Robert G. Cates, married Emily Jane Dalton who was related to the Dalton Gang.[79] The following explains: "It is interesting to note that the Daltons are said to be related to the Youngers who rode with Jesse James: Cole's (Younger) paternal great-great-grandfather had served with George Washington's army at Valley Forge, and his paternal great-grandmother was related to Revolutionary War general 'Light Horse Harry' Lee, father of Robert E. Lee. Cole's paternal grandfather, Charles Lee Younger, a native Virginian, emigrated first to Kentucky and then Missouri, where he became one of the wealthiest landowners in the western part of the state. (Charles sired nineteen children, including eleven who were illegitimate; one of the latter was Adeline Wilson, whose sons—Grat, Bob, and Emmett Dalton—were the Younger's cousins and would become notorious as the Dalton Gang."[80]

The above information supports the following posting on the Dalton Family Genealogy Forum: "The Dalton Boys' father was married to Adeline Younger, half sister to the Younger Boys' father, Henry Younger. They had the same father, Charles Younger, but different mothers. Charles was married to Henry's mother, but Adeline was his mistress."[81]

20. Chatman, Gilamore, and William Watson—Lived on Mustang Creek; a possible Jesse James connection. The Chatman my great-great-grandfather referred to may have been John Chatman, sometimes spelled Chapman, who was under Quantrill even though he was allegedly killed. The James-Younger Gang was a gang of American outlaws that included, but was not limited to, the Younger brothers, the James brothers, the Ford brothers, and the Chapman brothers. The Ford and Chapman brothers were never convicted.

The following Chapman is probably not who my great-great-grandfather referred to since he didn't live on Mustang Creek, but he was a veteran who enlisted in Falls County and either lived or was buried there post-Civil War, or he belonged to the Falls County Willis L. Lang Camp of Confederate Veterans:

Chapman, H. M., b.-, d.-, bur.-, Co E, 4 AL Inf: A.[82]

21. Clark, William Henry—A William Henry Clark allegedly rode with the James-Younger Gang. The following post on the internet mentions a Clark that rode with Jesse James being in Texas: "I'm very interested in the Clarks and the James Bros. My grandfather was Wm. Henry Clark born in SC abt. 1838. Rumor has it he was in the Civil War; he rode with the James bros. in Missouri and Texas, while living in AL (Alabama). It was told that Jesse James visited my grandfather in Dale county AL at one time."[83]

22. Clark, Jim—A possible Jesse James connection. Jim Cummins/ Cummings, a well-known James-Younger Gang member, used the alias of Jim Clark. *Branded as Rebels* relates the following information:

James Clark was born in Jackson County (Missouri) in 1841. He was a Quantrill man, joining him at the age of twenty. Supposed to have undertook many secret missions for Quantrill in the war. Killed at midnight, August 7, 1895 on Main Street in front of Columbia Saloon, Telluride, Colorado. He had gone to Telluride in 1887. Was serving as a law officer in Telluride, Colorado when mysteriously shot and killed. Ref: Atlanta Constitution dated August 1895 and letter from Chuck Parsons March 15, 1981. Account in the Lee's Summit Journal August 10, 1895, said he was also with the James Gang. He was shot from ambush. Said his mother lived in Jackson County. Spelled "Clark" in this account. His mother said he never drank or indulged in any excesses. According to Captain Langhorne and Marshal Whig Keshlear, Jim Clark was really Jim Cummins.[84]

However, Frank James did not believe that Jim Cummins was the sheriff of Telluride. An article from August 15, 1895, in the *McAlester Capital* explained:

Frank James does not believe that his old friend and pal, Jim Cummings, was shot at Telluride, Col., last Tuesday: "It's a thousand to one shot," said James to a Republic reporter yesterday, "that the City Marshal of Telluride, Jas. Clark, was not Jim Cummings. He may have been some Missouri Cummings, but I'm pretty sure it wasn't Jim. That man had too much sense to be City Marshal of any town. He couldn't possible have escaped recognition, out in that country because it is full of people who knew him in the old days and wouldn't hesitate to give him up in the hope of securing a reward. If I remember rightly there are a number of indictments hanging over Cummings."

Jim Cummings was born in Clay County, Missouri, 54 years ago, within three miles of the home of the James boys. Frank and Jesse James, Cummings, the Youngers and others of the band that became famous for its daring robberies in later years were boys and playmates together. When the war came on they espoused the cause of the Confederacy, and all enlisted in the company that was raised in Clay County and the bordering country by the notorious Quantrill. Cummings served through the war with Quantrell's raiders.

Shortly after the war Cummings was suspected of having robbed a bank at Liberty, but nothing could be prove against him. Later he was arrested for stealing horses, gave bond and jumped the bond. Then he joined the James boys and the Younger's, and was with them in nearly all their big jobs. When Cole and Jim Younger conceived the idea of going up to Northfield, Minn., to rob the bank there, Cummings opposed the project strenuously, but the sentiment of the gang was in favor of it, and the attempt was made with disastrous results that are a matter of history. Cummings refused to accompany the party.

When the James boys came back to Missouri after their awful fight and narrow escape from the Minnesota mob, Cummings joined the gang again. In 1879 or thereabouts, he, in company with Jesse James, Tucker Basham, Will Ryan and others, held up a Chicago and Alton train and furnished material for the history of the famous Glendale robbery. Shortly after this Cummings rode into Independence on horseback and consulted an attorney concerning his chances of getting clear of the charge of robbing the train, if he surrendered. The attorney assured him that conviction was certain. "Well, then," said Jim, "I'll leave the country."

He walked downstairs leisurely from the lawyer's office, mounted his horse and rode away. Since that time Jim Cummings has not been seen in Missouri. Frank James thoughtfully spat on the ground yesterday and remarked, quietly: "That couldn't have been Jim. You see, Jim was one of those men that won't let anybody shoot him."[85]

Or the Jim Clark my great-great-grandfather referred to may have been James Clark, a white male born in Mississippi but living in Marlin, Falls County, Texas, at the age of twenty-one in 1870.[86] If so, he assumed the alias of Jim Snodgrass and may have robbed a Louisiana stagecoach.

23. Clark, John—A Union soldier during the Civil War: "Massachusetts, Acting Master (Ensign), U. S. Navy. Served as a doctor 1862–1865 on ships such as USS Preble, Potomac, Calhoun."[87] Further details of him follow:

Dr. John S. Clark was born April 18, 1823 in Bristol England and died April 4, 1888 and is buried in Blevins Cemetery. He married Pricilla Prichard on July 8, 1844 in Bristol England. He was an Ensign in the U.S. Navy from Sept. 1862 to Nov. 16, 1865. He came to Falls County in December of 1872. Records of his marriage are at the Parish of St. Thomas Church in Bristol. His father was James and listed as a laborer. John S. lived in Braintree, Mass. until 1866 and then moved to Franklin Co, Mo. in 1871 before coming to Texas. Five sons were born of this marriage; John Jr., Frank, Ben, George A. and Charlie Fitch—the youngest who was born Oct. 17, 1859. Records indicate he was a Mariner.[88]

Clark's granddaughter, Lucille Clark Harris, related the following: "Our grandfather Clark was known as a doctor but there are no records to establish this fact." And, "enough information has been verified to get a Civil War marker on his gravesite."[89]

According to our relative Mae Courtney Thompson, my great-great-grandfather and John S. Clark did not get along. My great-great-grandfather referred to him as "Old Man Clark." Mae wrote:

A jealous neighbor, John Clark, who had been camping on the "wrong" side of the creek, turned Grandpa Courtney in for carrying a pistol—which was against the law in post-Civil War Texas. Grandpa was charged with threatening Mr. Clark with the pistol for trespassing, and his diary indicated he was afraid of Clark starting a prairie fire. For several months, Grandpa Courtney avoided the Sheriff so as not to receive the "summons" for a hearing. He was, however, finally tried and jailed for nine months.[90]

I searched the criminal records of the Falls County Courthouse in Marlin, Texas, at least three times and did not find any record on James L. Courtney. If he was gone from home for nine months, what was he really doing? Jesse James's little half-brother, Archie Payton Samuel, was killed on January 26, 1875. Oddly enough my great-great-grandfather didn't make any diary entries at all from December 23, 1874 through July 5, 1876. On December 21, 1874, he wrote, "at dark Shelton he came & he said the sherif was after me & the offence was worse than jail." He obviously wasn't in jail as evidenced by the lack of a record. Could he have been on the run from the law and then got word that his family had been attacked by the Pinkerton group of detectives and headed for Missouri?

I believe that the trouble between my great-great-grandfather and "Old Man Clark" can be attributed to the fact that they fought on opposite sides during the Civil War—Clark for the North and my great-great-grandfather for the South.

24. Mr. Coal—My great-great-grandfather knew a Dan F. Cole (listed below) but I doubt that he referred to him as "Mr. Coal" because he spelled the two names differently, Coal and Cole. I could find no surname spelled as Coal, so maybe he resorted to his common practice of using nicknames and dubbed someone "Mr. Coal." Jesse James's mother is said to have called Frank James "Mr. Frank."[91] Maybe my great-great-grandfather referred to Cole Younger as Mr. Coal, although Cole Younger was nicknamed Bud.

25. Cole, Dan F.—"Daniel was born about 1845 in Mississippi to Elizabeth Cole, born about 1803 in South Carolina, and her unknown husband who had lived in Tennessee before settling in Mississippi."[92] (Please see also information for Daniel M. Jackson.)

Daniel F. Cole married Mary Emily Bull (born in 1855 in Yazoo County Mississippi) on January 25, 1870, in Falls Country, Texas.[93]

D. F. Cole was a Freemason belonging to Carolina Lodge, No. 330, District 17 along with my great-great-grandfather.[94]

Jesse James's mother's maiden name was Cole but I haven't yet determined if Dan F. Cole was related to her. Frank and Jesse James's maternal uncle was Jesse Richard Cole of Clay County, Missouri, who married Louisa Eleanor Maret.[95] Louisa was Archibald Clinton Courtney, Sr.'s daughter.

26. Conley, Sam—A possible James-Younger Gang connection. Steve Wilson, author of *Oklahoma Treasures and Treasure Tales,* relates that "a man identified only as Conley spoke often of Frank and Jesse James and is believed to have been a lookout man for them. He is said to have talked like he must have been there and he had a cowhide (treasure) map which he said was only one of three copies."[96]

My great-great-grandfather's diaries indicate that he often "grained a cow hide or sometimes just half a hide." I assume "graining" meant he was tanning the hides to make them soft and pliable for various uses including making treasure maps.

Census records for 1880 indicate there was a W. S. Conoly in Falls County.

27. Cooper—May have been the Ben Cooper who was credited as a member of the gang that carried out the Clay County Savings Association robbery in Liberty, Missouri, which was attributed to the James-Younger Gang.[97]

Branded as Rebels reports that "Benjamin Cooper joined Company 1, 5th Regimental Cavalry, under Gordon." According to Rose Mary Lankford's *The Encyclopedia of Quantrill's Guerrillas,* Gordon was the "Silas Gordon who rode with Quantrill." She also reported that he was a suspect in the Liberty Bank robbery, the first robbery accredited to the James-Younger Gang.

It is interesting to note that a Benjamin Cooper from Missouri was living in McLennan County, Texas (which adjoins Falls County, where Jesse lived), in 1870. The city of Waco is the county seat of McLennan County.[98]

Or the Cooper my great-great-grandfather referred to may have been one of the following Coopers residing in Falls County, Texas, in 1870, according to the census records of that year given on Ancestry.com:

David Cooper Precinct 2, Falls, TX 28 1841 Louisiana White Male; Pinkney Cooper Precinct 2, Falls, TX 27 1842 North

Carolina White Male; Brown Cooper Precinct 5, Falls, TX 19 1850
Mississippi White Male; Hiram Cooper Precinct 5, Falls, TX 24
1845 Mississippi White Male[99]

28. Courtney, Mary Ellen Barron—My great-great-grandmother.
Mary Ellen was the daughter of Thomas Hudson Barron and Mary
Jane Shelton, and wife of Jesse James a.k.a. James L. Courtney. She was
born October 19, 1854, on Barron Branch at the old Barron residence
in Waco before her parents relocated in Blevins, Falls County, Texas.
She and my great-great-grandfather married on October 31, 1871. Mary
Ellen died on October 21, 1910, and is buried in the Blevins Cemetery.
She is said to have been devoutly religious.

29. Cox, Tom—Elias Tom Cox was forty-one years old and living
in McLennan County in 1870. He was born on October 2, 1829, in
Tennessee and died in McLennan County, Texas. Tom Cox Cemetery in
McLennan County, Texas, was named for him. He was a 2nd Lieutenant
of 2nd Company raised in Bell County Texas for the Confederate service, exempt from active duty because of one crippled foot.

My relative Mae Courtney Thompson said that my great-great-
grandfather and Tom Cox didn't get along very well. I have a feeling
the following story explains why:

During the war, bushwhackers, army deserters and other bad and
dangerous characters drifted into this part of the country. At this
time, E. Tom Cox, a great hunter, lived at Mastersville (now called
Eddy). One of his neighbors, Henry Williams owned a few negroes.
Cox and Williams trained the dogs by having them run one of these
negroes. These dogs were very useful in deer hunts. In a deer hunt,
old Roller, the leader of the pack, chased the deer into the hidden
camp of these outlaws in one of the upper marsh thickets on South
Cow Bayou. The outlaws recognized the dog as being one of Tom
Cox's "negro dogs" and killed him. They decided that Cox was out

after them with the dogs, so they sent him a warning note, which was dropped in a store in Waco village where Cox and Williams were known to trade. The note stated: "We have heard and we know you have been hunting and trying to run us [down?] with 'negro dogs'. So we are sending you this note and now warning you that if you three D—D—D—don't leave this county and that at once, we will shoot your d----- hides so full of holes that they won't hold corn shucks." This open note was signed by a dozen of these known bad men. The store keeper put a boy on a horse to take the note to Cox and Williams and their close companion, Bill Long.

They decided they must answer the note. To be sure that their reply was received by the bad men, they sent it direct to their camp. The outlaws had moved their camp to the thickets of Owl Creek beyond the Leon River. The answer was addressed to the signers of the threatening note. The answer was: "We have received the note dropped by you and signed by several of you. Answering the same, we wish to say that we have not been hunting you with negro dogs, or in any way hunting you or meddling with you or any of your sort. We are living here, as you know, have our families here and all we have is here. We did not come here to be run off and we are not going and all we ask of you is not to shoot from behind a tree." This was signed by [Tom?] Cox, Henry Williams, and Bill Long. Three men against dozens of outlaws. The friends went armed and met often to talk over the situation.[100]

30. Crow, H. S.—On March 20, 1871, my great-great-grandfather wrote that he received a letter from H. S. Crow dated March 2, 1871. Then on August 12, 1871, he wrote that he went "ahunting with Crow, Bud Singleton [a known member of the James-Younger Gang], and Barron." The 1860 census shows the following information:

Name: H S Crow
Age in 1860: 10

Birth Year: abt 1850

Birthplace: South Carolina

Home in 1860: Ward 4, Claiborne, Louisiana

Gender: Male

Post Office: Flat Lick

Household Members by Name and Age: John Crow 63; M Crow 44; Robert Crow 24; J J Crow 22; D Mc Crow 21; Thos Crow 17; M L Crow 13; H S Crow 10; W W Crow 8; S A Crow 6; L L Crow 2.

H. S. Crow employed black men who registered for the World War I draft in DeSoto Parish, Louisiana.[101]

According to the Louisiana Statewide Death Index, 1900–1949 the initials H. S. stood for Henry Stevens:

Name: Henry Stevens Crow; Death Date: 19 Jan 1921; Estimated birth year: 1850; Age: 71 years; Parish: Desoto; Certificate Number: 245; Volume: 1; Title: Louisiana Statewide Death Indexes 1900–1929.

Census records for 1920 list a Henry S. Crow, age seventy, a white male born in South Carolina but living in the 7th WD of De Soto Parish, Louisiana. As is written in the *Cemetery Book* by Amos Barron, "H. S. Crow is buried in Wallace Cemetery, DeSoto Parish, Louisiana."[102]

31. Crowley—May have been the Francis M. Crowly from Missouri who was living in Jeremiah Amos Burnett's household in Denton, Texas, in 1860. My great-great-grandfather also mentioned a Burnett living on Denton Creek in his diary. One online source tells that:

Jeremiah Burnett's home was destroyed during the bloody Ruffian and Jayhawker raids in 1857 and 1858. The family pulled up stakes and headed south, settling in Denton County, Texas. [Listed in the

1860 census is]: Burnett, Jeremiah, 36, Stock raiser, $1600, $3100, MO; Nancy, 31, Virginia; Samuel B., 11, MO; Tillman H., 10, MO; Mary A., 7, MO; Phoenix M., 5, MO; Melinda E., 3, MO; Jeremiah, 1, MO; and Crowly, Francis M., 25, Farmer, MO.[103]

An excerpt from postings made on the Cates Family Genealogy Forum on the internet reported that there is a James-Younger-Dalton connection through the Crowleys (written verbatim):

Mary Frances Crowley, born 1845 in Missouri was married to William Andrew Cates, born 1850 in Texas; married 9 Sept 1869; died 4 Nov 1927. I have her line going back quite a ways but it is quite extensive as it goes back 12 generations from her. I do NOT have it verified. I am working on it. And through this line there is a relation to the Younger Gang, the Dalton Gang and a slight relation (through marriage) to the James gang as follows:

Mary Frances Crowley was the Daughter of Louisa Jane Younger. Her Father was Richard Younger (Married to Nancy Ann Horn). Richard was the son of Captain Henry W. Younger and Sarah Anderson (Heathman-1st marriage). Henry's Brother was Charles Lee Younger. Now Charles Lee had MANY MANY wives. In fact there were 5 of them—with a total of like 22 children. Anyways from his 2nd wife. He had a daughter by the name of Adeline Lee Younger. She married James Lewis Dalton Jr. and was the mother of the Dalton Gang. I don't have all of their names yet. Ok, From Charles Lee's 5th Wife (Sarah Sulivan Purcell) You Find Thomas Coleman Younger. He had 3 wives. His 3rd was Augusta Peters (Inskip-first marriage). Her Mother, Frances Simms, had a brother by the name of Benjamin Simms. He was Married to Zerelda Cole. She was the Mother to Jesse and Frank James, our famous outlaws. So Benjamin is the Step-Father to these boys. Like I said only a slight relation via marriage. Unless I can find something through the Dalton Line. I was told there was one, but I haven't found it yet.

Now, supposedly, Augusta Peters had a sister named Mary Peters. She married a man named Martin Ringo. They had a son—Johnny Ringo. The Gunfighter.

Now Charles Lee Younger also had another son, by the name of Henry Washington Younger, from Sarah. Henry was the Father to four children. Coleman, Robert, Henrietta, and James. Also known as Cole, Bob, and Jim Younger. A.K.A. The Younger gang.

I don't have the source information in front of me, but it is from a book on the Younger family genealogy. All except the information on Johnny Ringo. Someone passed it on.[104]

32. Crudup, Bob—Census records indicate that Robert Crudup was born in Tennessee in 1860 but later lived in McLennan County, Waco, Texas.

The following is written verbatim in the "Genealogy Records Collection of Robert Powell Carver" on Rootsweb:

Robert Crudup married: (1) Mary Guill; (2) Carolina Steele Harkreader; and (3) Almedia Barron. The first two marriages occurred in Wilson Co., TN and the third in TX. He moved from Wilson Co TN to Perry Co. where he was State Representative, then on to Dyer Co, and finally to TX, where he died as a member of the TX State Legislature. From 1843–1845 Robert Crudup represented Perry County in 25th Tennessee General Assembly. Represented Falls, Limestone, and McLennan Counties (District 19) in 12th Texas Legislature. Robert Crudup, Chief Justice of McLennan County, and Representative to 12th Texas Legislature. Crudup died in office on July 13, 1870 and is buried in Texas State Cemetery Austin, Texas.[105]

Robert Crudup knew Thomas H. Barron when he was a Texas Ranger: "Robert Crudup bought a parcel of land from Thomas Barron, who was a Texas Ranger at the time. Robert Crudup's plot was just off the courthouse square next to the Brazos River. When he sold the land to the town he put a clause in the contract that no improvements could be made or no building could be erected until the year 2000. Today, it's a city park just west of the courthouse square."[106]

Another source related the following: "The land that Robert Crudup gave to the City of Waco was some of the best cotton land on the river. Family legend has it that Robert Crudup put the stipulations on the land because of the 'Carpet Baggers' that were taking over any property that was along the river."[107]

33. Cunningham, John—Census records show that in 1870 John Cunningham from Pennsylvania was living in the household of James Vestal in Waco, Texas. Permelia Vestal Densman was also living there. A James and Bill Cunningham were with Quantrill.[108] Was John Cunningham, who eventually married Permelia, related to them? The Vestals had ties to Missouri and Jesse James.

> Permelia Vestal, daughter of Joab Vestal and Sophronia Spencer Vestal, married Harris D. Record, and their daughter, Mary Melissa Record, married John Evans Cunningham [see Vestal surname, p. 158].

John Cunningham may have been related to the William C. "Cleb" Cunningham from Missouri that married Almeda Barron, one of Thomas Hudson Barron's daughters:

> William C. "Cleb" Cunningham; Born – Abt 1827 MO; Died – 15 Feb 1853 Falls Co., TX; Census Milam Co., TX 1850 (p 13); DEATH: Courtney. Diary/day book of Thomas H. Barron; sp-Almeda Olivia Barron, Dau of Thomas Hudson Barron (War 1812) & Elizabeth Carnall. Census: Milam Co., TX 1850.[109]

34. Dad—My great-great-grandfather sometimes referred to Thomas H. Barron, his wife's father, as "Dad." He also referred to someone else as "Dad" because he did so after Thomas H. Barron died on February 24, 1874. According to the oral and written family history of Mae Courtney Thompson, my great-great-grandfather never spoke of his own parents so it may never be known who "Dad" was.

35. Davis, B.M.L.—Possibly connected to the James-Younger and Dalton gangs. According to my great-great-grandfather, B.M.L. Davis lived in New Albany, Kansas, which is approximately forty miles north-northwest of Coffeyville, Kansas, where the notorious Dalton Gang lived. According to the following posting by Walt Nichols, Davises in the New Albany area were connected to the Dalton Gang:

> Alonzo Davis – KS/CO 1880s–1920s. Notes for ALONZO PHINEAS 'AP' DAVIS: My dad (Bryan Nichols) said: "the Davis' were friends of or somehow related to the Dalton family around Coffeyville, Kansas. After the Dalton Gang's famous holdup (1892) in Coffeyville, the Davis' were no longer welcome around there so they moved to Colorado." Dad also said "The Dalton's were not too bad . . . but the Younger's were just plain mean." This must have came from his granddad, AP Davis. I believe my dad's mother (Hattie Adeline Davis Nichols) born in Coffeyville seven years before the holdup, was named for the mother of the Dalton boys (Adeline Lee [Younger] Dalton). She was related to Cole Younger. I believe the youngest Dalton girl (Hannah Adeline Dalton) was named for my dad's grandmother (Hannah Alamira [Walker] Davis). The Dalton's oldest son was named Charles Benjamin Dalton. The Davis' youngest son was named Benjamin 'Bennie' Davis, born in Coffeyville three years before the holdup. The Davis' also had a son Charles.[110]

In another posting about Alonzo Davis, Nichols relates that the Dalton Gang spent the night at the Davis Farm: "I just found a very interesting web-site [no longer accessible]. It mentions how the Dalton

Gang stayed the night at the Davis farm. They call it the P. L. Davis farm, that's wrong . . . that was my great-grandfather, A.P. Davis."[111]

36. Devers—May have been the James "Jim" Devers who rode with Jesse James and was in Texas after the Civil War.

The Devers my great-great-grandfather mentioned was more than likely one of the Devers families from Clay County, Missouri, or related to them. The Devers, James, Courtneys, Pences, and Marets are all related. (Merrit is a variant spelling for Maret).[112] This is validated by the Mid-Missouri Genealogical Society, Inc., in the *Pioneer Times* in a 1986 article titled, "The Courtney's [*sic*] of Clay County," submitted by Wilrena Calvert Miller: "A. C. Courtney, Sr. spent his 86th birthday on 1 May 1900, at Kearney at the home of his daughter, Mrs. Jane Maret." Census records indicate that there were no Devers in Falls County, Texas (where my great-great-grandfather lived). The Devers living closest to Falls County follow:

- Devers, Archibald, Age: 25, Male, White, Born: TN, Living in TX, Erath Co., Stephenville, P O [Box] 1870
- Devers, Elizabeth, Age: 27, Female, White, Born: MO, Living in TX, Williamson Co., Round Rock P O [Box] 1870[113]

The following posting from the Maret Family Genealogy Forum relates information about the James "Jim" Devers who rode with Jesse James:

Jim Devers, a son of John & Nancy Devers, was with the James gang, was captured by authorities when he visited relatives in KY, and was taken back to Missouri and hanged. I found information on the internet about a James M. Devers, believed to be a member of the James gang who was arrested in Kentucky and brought to Missouri where he was lodged in the Richmond jail. On March 17, 1868 about fifteen men removed him from the jail and hanged him. This story sounds very much like the Maret family story except, based on the date, it would probably mean that he would have been a grandson rather than son of John Devers and Nancy Merrit.[114]

James Devers, Alva Devers, Arthur "Art" Devers, and Alexander Devers all served under Captain George Todd who was with Quantrill. Arthur and James went to Texas during the Civil War with George Shepard.[115]

Branded as Rebels reports that Alexander and Arthur "Art" Devers from Clay County, Missouri, were both killed on March 30, 1865, in the northern part of Clay County, Missouri, at the residence of a Mrs. Fox. Both men were buried in the same grave.[116] Genealogical information for Alexander follows:

Name: Alexander Devers

Birth: ABT 1814 in Crab Orchard/Lincoln Kentucky

Death: 1880 in Daviess County, Missouri

Residence: 1870 Miller, Gentry, Missouri

Residence: 1860 Township 61, Gentry, Missouri

Father: John Devers

Mother: Nancy Merrit

Marriage 1 Penelope b: ABT 1814 in Kentucky

Children: Arthur Devers b: 1835 in Kentucky; Alva Merret Devers b: APR 1836; Kentucky; Elizabeth Devers b: 1839 in Kentucky; James Devers b: 1839 in Kentucky; Alexander Devers b: 1848 in Kentucky; William Devers b: 1849 in Missouri; Archibald Devers b: 1853 in Missouri; Sarah J Devers b: 1855 in Missouri; Robert Devers b: 1857 in Missouri; Sarah M Devers b: 1859 in Missouri; and Mary A Devers b: 1861 in Missouri.[117]

37. Elison—According to his diary, on September 13, 1871, my great-great-grandfather "went to Elison's for a dance and danced all night." Elison may have been:

William Ellison; Age in 1870: 21; Estimated Birth Year: 1848; Birthplace: Mississippi; Home in 1870: Precinct 2, Falls, Texas; Race: White; Gender: Male; Post Office: Marlin; Roll: M593_1584; Page: 27; Image: 53; Year: 1870.[118]

Another source says he was living in the household of Samuel Wilson, was twenty-one years old, and from Mississippi.[119]

Michael Ellison responded to a message I posted on the Ellison Family Genealogy Forum (written verbatim):

> I am not necessarily related to William Ellison. His family owned my ancestors, and when my people were freed they kept the Ellison last name. I do know that the Ellison men did fight for the Confederacy in the Civil War, and the Company out of Lockhart Texas was commanded by an Ellison. The Ellison's were one of the largest cattle movers up the Chisholm Trail, and they came to TX in 1847 with President LBJ's [Lyndon Baines Johnson's] relatives in a covered wagon convoy from Mississippi. William's father was Nathaniel Ellison. They all settled in Caldwell County, Texas in Lockhart and Luling. Nearly all Ellison's, black or white, in Texas are traced back to this family.[120]

Or the Ellison my great-great-grandfather referred to may have been A. P. Ellison, a veteran who enlisted in Falls Co.; lived or was buried there post-Civil War; or belonged to the Falls Co. Willis L. Lang Camp of Confederate Veterans:

> Ellison, A. P., b. 1819, d. 1872, bur. P. Chapel Cem, Co C, 15 AL Inf.[121]

38. Erven, Jim—Also spelled Ervin. Census records indicate that a J. W. Ervin from Missouri lived in Falls County, Texas in 1880:

> Ervin J W; Age: 32; Sex: M; Race: W; Place of Birth: Missouri; Place of Residence in 1880: TX Falls County 5-PCT 1880.

I suspect that Jim Erven may have been related to the John Erven/ Ervin who rode with Quantrill and later the James Gang. He attended the 1921 Quantrill Reunion and was at the second burial of the purported body of Jesse James in 1902.[122]

John Ervin may have been:

John Chalmers Ervin, Born Aug 5, 1847. Was captured April 1864 at Lexington and held prisoner. A woman (supposedly Anna Fickle) was caught trying to break him out. She was sentenced to 3 yrs in prison. Survived the war and settled in Marshall, MO. Was at JJ (Jesse James') 2nd funeral in 1882. Attended reunions from 1901 to 1921 (would very rarely miss one) Died March 24, 1924, and buried at Ridge Park Cemetery, Marshall, MO. His grave is marked only with a metal military marker. He also had a brother named Hence (nickname?) Ervin.[123]

39. Farley—May have been the Jesse Farley who died in Bell County, Texas. (Bell County joins Falls County near my great-great-grandfather's former residence.)

Birth: 1833 in White Co., TN; Death: 1906 in Bell Co, TX. Father: William Thomas Farley b: 1798 in NC; Mother: Eliza B. Yeager b: ABT 1800 in TN. Married: Mary Jane Clary 24 OCT 1857 in Washington Co, AR Children: Frances Farley b: 1858 in AR; Mary Farley b: 1862 in AR; Jesse L. Farley b: 1864 in AR; and James F. Farley b: 1866 in TX.[124]

Farleys were connected to Jesse James: "Thaddeous Farley was with Silas Gordon's Company January 16, 1862."[125] James Farley lived in Clay County, Missouri, (where Jesse James was born and raised) in 1860: "James Farley; Age 25; White male; Born in Ireland but living in Gallatin Township, Clay County, Missouri in 1860."[126]

A bit of Civil War trivia: "April 12: At 4:30 a.m., under General Beauregard's orders, Captain George S. James gave the order to fire the signal shot which would also open fire on Sumter. Lieutenant Henry S. Farley fired the first official shot which started the American Civil War."[127]

40. Fontenot, G.—Gervais Fontenot was a retired U.S. marshal and the nephew of the famous pirate, Jean Lafitte. Recall that my great-great-grandfather stayed overnight at G. Fontenot's place during a trip to Louisiana. My great-great-grandfather and Jim Cummins a.k.a. Jim Clark a.k.a. Jim Snodgrass stayed overnight at G. Fontenot's house on January 7, 1874, during their trip to Louisiana. He wrote that "Bud had put up at the same house" (G. Fontenot's house). The "Bud" he was referring to may have been Cole Younger because Cole himself said he was in Louisiana on that date (see information on Jim Clark listed above regarding the trip to Louisiana and subsequent stagecoach robbery).

Reggie Anne Walker-Wyatt, author of *Chasing Rivers, Trains, and Jesse James*, wrote that Gerasime Fontenot rode with Jesse James. Census Records indicate that the G. Fontenot my great-great-grandfather referred to may have been Gerasime L. Fontenot, twenty-three years old at the time of the 1870 census. He was a white male, born in Louisiana and living in St. Landry Parish, Ward Three, Louisiana.

Or G. Fontenot may have been Alphonse G. Fontenot:

Alphonse G. Fontenot; Birth: About 1843 in Opelousas, St Landry Parish, Louisiana; Death: ABT 1904 in Opelousas, St. Landry Parish, Louisiana; Marriage 1 Vaenez M. 'Vienna' Lee b: 12 NOV 1845 in Opelousas, St Landry Parish, Louisiana. Married: 5 DEC 1865 in Opelousas, St Landry Parish, Louisiana; Children: Oscar Fontenot b: 2 NOV 1872 in Washington, St. Landry Parish, Louisiana. . . . A. G. Fontenot served the Confederacy as a private in 28 (Thomas') Louisiana Infantry.[128]

Carol Holmes wrote the following information regarding Alphonse:

If Alphonse G. Fontenot is the same Fontenot as mentioned in the diary, more of the mystery comes to life. Alphonse G. Fontenot married Vaenez "Vinnie" Lee. Vinnie Lee is the daughter of George Miles Lee and Sophie Smith. George Miles Lee Jr. is the son of George Miles Lee Sr. and Rachel Clark born 1797 Baltimore, Maryland. Rachel Clark is the daughter of John K Clark born 1773 in Baltimore. John Clark married Celeste "Sarah" Roberts. Celeste Sarah Roberts is the daughter of Benjamin Roberts born 1740 in Wales and Elizabeth Cole born 1739 in Pa.

41. Galloway—The Reverend Robert Sallee James, Frank and Jesse James's father, mentioned the Galloways of Clay County, Missouri in a letter to his wife. Rev. and Mrs. James, along with their children, Frank, Jesse, and Susan, lived in Clay County, Missouri. In 1850 Robert James left with a wagon train headed for the gold fields of California and upon his arrival to Sacramento he wrote a letter to his wife, Zerelda, that he found two of the Galloways from Clay County already there: "Sacramento City, California, July 19, 1850: I found several of the Clay County boys viz. John Martin; J. King; L, ___; and the 2 Galloways."[129]

42. Galloway, John—"Galloway, John; Age 53; White male; Born in Illinois; Lived in Marlin, Falls County, Texas in 1870."[130]

Father: Adam Galloway b: 1790 in Kentucky or Tennessee; Mother: Sarah LEECH b: 1795; Marriage 1 Elizabeth (?) Galloway b: 1823 in Tennessee Married: ABT 1840 in Effingham, Illinois; Children: Adam Galloway b: 1841 in Effingham, Illinois; Female Galloway b: ABT 1845; Sarah Galloway b: 11 Dec 1847 in Jefferson Co., Illinois; John Sidney Galloway b: 10 May 1850 in Jefferson Co., Illinois; David Galloway b: 1852 in Arkansas; Benjamin P. Galloway b: 1855 in Texas; Seth Galloway b: 1 Apr 1858 in Texas; Lucinda Galloway b: Mar 1860 in Bosqueville, McLennan, Texas.[131]

43. Gordon—A possible Quantrill connection.

May have been Silas "Cy" or "Si" Gordon who rode with Quantrill. Some sources say he was killed in 1864, while other sources claim he was in Texas after the Civil War, which ended in 1865.[132] Civil War muster rolls list Gordon Silas; M.; I 1 Missouri Cavalry; Captain. Silas Gordon is said to have been born 2 April 1835 in Clark County, Kentucky and died in Grayson County, Texas. His father was William Gordon, born December 24, 1794, in Goochland County, Kentucky, and his mother was Lucretia Muir, born July 1794 in Clark County, Kentucky.[133]

History of Grayson County, Texas describes the town bearing his family's name:

Gordonville (Texas) is on Farm Road 901 and the shores of Lake Texoma twelve miles north of Whitesboro in the northwest corner of Grayson County. It was a part of Holford's sheep ranch until 1872, when Mark Clayton selected it for the site of his general store. William Clarke Quantrill and his guerrillas camped in that secluded area on their frequent visits to Grayson County during the Civil War. Quantrill's treasurer was Capt. Silas M. Gordon, after whom the Gordonville post office was named. When Quantrill left Grayson County for good, Gordon remained behind and operated a trading post in the new town. The Gordonville post office is one of the oldest in the county. The town's population reached its peak of 300 in 1925. In the 1940s the Gordonville School was consolidated with that of Whitesboro. After World War II the population declined. In 1949 Gordonville had a population of 200 and six businesses. In 1989 the community had Baptist and Presbyterian churches and eighteen businesses serving the growing community near Lake Texoma. In 1990 the recorded population in Gordonville was 220.[134]

The following posting was made on the Gordon Family Genealogy Forum:

Cyrus or Silas Gordon was with Quantrill. On August 12, 1861, it was reported that he had enlisted companies in Platte Co, MO. for the Confederacy. On Sept 16 1981, he and his Lt., Black Triplett, went out to the stream saw mill on the turnpike near Platte City to meet Col. R.P. Smith of the 16th Illinois Infantry who were on the way to the aid of Col. Mulligan at Lexington, Missouri. Smith had 300 men and one cannon and they were from St. Joseph. In the battle a physician from St. Joe was killed. The confederate force won the battle and looted the town of Platte City. In Dec 1861, Gordon was back in Platte City where his men were camped on the public Square. On Jan 16 1862, Silas' company was sworn in at Springfield. Mo and was designated as the 9th Co., Col. Gates Regiment, 1st Brigade of Missouri Volunteers under Gov. Jackson's call. The list of members was found in the Border Times of March 16, 1866 and it said that Silas was captured and paroled at Vicksburg. On Oct 6, 1862, it was reported that Silas Gordon, Boaz Roberts, Quantrill were topics in Platte CO. Other accounts said that he was with Quantrill at Centralia, Sept 27 1864; Baxter Springs, Oct 3 1863. Killed in 1864. Gordon was reported living in Texas by Paxton in 1897. Gordon was the son of William Gordon (died August 1841) and Lucretia Gordon (Died Feb 10 1864).[135]

Or the Gordon my great-great-grandfather referred to may have been Thomas Tolson Gordon, but he was a Union soldier.

Gordon, Thomas Tolson, b. 19 Nov 1844, d. 5 Oct 1923, bur. Union Cem, Sgt, 53 AL Cav.[136]

44. Gordang, William—My great-great-grandfather noted in his diary that William Gordang lived on the Colorado River and that it was one stack from Stephenville to Colorado River.* "Gordang" may

---

*A *stack* is a surveyor's term.

have been a nickname for Gordon—my great-great-grandfather was known for nicknaming people. Sixteen-year-old William Gordon was living in the household of the Silas Gordon, listed above, in 1870.

A William Gordon also lived in Erath County, Texas:

William Riley Gordon; Birth: 15 Nov 1845 in Missouri; Death: in Texas; Father: William Gordon; born ca 1808 in Georgia; Mother: Lucinda (Lucy) LEWELLEN b: 1825 in N.C.; Marriage 1 Lidia Ellen Fiveash; b: 1 Nov 1851 in Cherokee, Texas; Children: Eight[137]

45. Harding, James (Harden/Hardin)—A possible James-Younger Gang connection. The following posting on the Harding Family Genealogy Forum may be referring to the James Harding who rode with Jesse James because aliases are being used. This particular James Harding has Missouri and Texas connections living in McLennan County, which adjoins Falls County, Texas, where my great-great-grandfather lived:

James D. Harding a.k.a. Witter Hardin/Harden: On the 1850 Cedar Co. MO census, he is shown as "Witter." The 1860 McLennan County, Texas census records lists him as James Hardin, and then later as James D. Harding. Father was James Hardin, b. 1801-TN who was in AR (Crawford Co/Clark Co). Family migrated back and forth from Cedar Co. MO to AR area and then to McLennan Co. Texas by 1853 or so.[138]

The 1860 Federal Census for McLennan County, Texas shows a:

James D Harding; Age in 1860: 18; Birthplace: Arkansas; Home in 1860: Not Stated, McLennan, Texas; Gender: Male; Post Office: Bold Springs; Roll: M653_1300; Page: 418; Year: 1860; Head of Household: Jane Cox.[139]

It's also interesting to note that James Hardin Younger a.k.a. Jim Younger used the alias of James "Jim" Hardin. He may have participated in the following bank robberies: Liberty, Missouri Bank Robbery; Adair, Iowa Train Robbery; and Northfield, Minnesota Bank Robbery.[140]

Or perhaps the James Harding my great-great-grandfather mentioned was the Joseph James Hardin who rode with Quantrill. He was with Quantrill and Fletch Taylor, a Captain under Quantrill. As is the case with many other ex-Quantrill Raiders and members of the James Gang, confusion surrounds his date of death: "Killed by Missouri State Militia February 10, 1863 in Platte County. Gregg said it was February 11. Brownlee said Hardin was killed in 1862."[141]

46. Haun, T. N.—Theodore Napoleon Haun was really Theodore Napoleon Courtney but changed his name to Haun sometime between 1867 and 1870.[142] He was allegedly the real James L. Courtney's brother. However, my great-great-grandfather, known as James L. Courtney in Texas, referred to Theodore Napoleon Haun as his cousin: "January 23, 1872: Sunday morning at Barron's and remained there all day & rote to leters one to Rat and the other to cousin Theodore & Miley was here."[143]

Carol Holmes has consulted genealogical records and verified that the Courtneys a.k.a. Hauns were cousins of Jesse James, which explains why my great-great-grandfather referred to Theodore Courtney a.k.a. Theodore Haun as his cousin instead of his brother.

Theodore N. Courtney a.k.a. Theodore Napoleon Haun: Birth: 16 AUG 1850 near Nashville, Davidson Co., Tennessee; Death: 20 FEB 1934 in Parkerville, Morris Co., Kansas; Father: Stephen Courtney b: 1 OCT 1822 in Greene Co., Tennessee; Mother: Diana Dorthulla Andruss b: 29 SEP 1821 in Jefferson Co., Tennessee; Marriage 1 Priscilla Margaret Ramsey b: 9 MAR 1858 in Nainsville, Clinton Co.; Missouri; Married: 21 JAN 1875 in Parkerville, Morris Co., Kansas; Marriage 2 Elizabeth Skaggs born: Unknown; Married: Unknown.[144]

Jesse James's mother and other family members may have stayed in Morris County, Texas, after Jesse left for Texas. Another item of interest that may connect the Courtney a.k.a. Haun family to the Wilkersons, who rode with Jesse James, is evidenced by the 1880 census for Morris County, Kansas. The census lists James and E. Wilkinson/ Wilkerson as wards of the Courtneys a.k.a. Hauns. John Courtney a.k.a. John Haun married second to E. Wilkerson. Knowing the family story and knowing that something appears to have made the Courtneys a.k.a. Hauns run from the law, I wouldn't doubt that the Wilkersons living with them were related to the James and Bill Wilkerson who rode with Jesse James. Was the Courtney a.k.a. Haun household one of the James-Younger Gang's hideouts?

47. Hines—A possible Jesse James connection. My great-great-grandfather hunted for horses with "Cooper & Hines" on April 2, 1872. Was this Hines the same James "Jim" Hines who rode with the James-Younger Gang and went to Texas after the Civil War? "Jim Cummins lists Jim Hines as being a member of the James gang and living on a cattle ranch in Texas. This could be John Hines."[145] *Branded as Rebels* lists "John or (Jack?) Hines as being with Jesse James (?) after the war."[146]

Lankford cites *Branded as Rebels* as reporting that "James O. Hinds, Jr. (Hines?) was a suspect in the Muncie, Kansas, train robbery which was committed by the James-Younger Gang. Hinds was arrested by the Deputy Marshal Hampton at Mrs. Burn's home near Independence, and was saved by Jesse James. He later wrote a letter to the Kansas City Journal stating his innocence and claiming Jesse James did not rescue him."[147]

Jesse James is related to the Hineses as Mary Hines was his direct paternal ancestor. "William James married Mary Hines on July 15, 1774 in Virginia."[148]

Maybe the James "Jim" Hines listed as follows who is buried at Pack Saddle Mountain was the same James "Jim" Hines who rode with Jesse

James. Legend has it that treasure is buried around this mountain—maybe the James-Younger Gang buried some of their loot there.

> Name: James L. Hines; Birth: 23 SEP 1842 in Ozark, Missouri; Death: 6 NOV 1885; Burial: Old Montgomery Ranch, Pack Saddle, Llano, Texas; Father: Jacob Hines b: Abt 1811 in Ohio; Mother: Sarah Noble b: 29 OCT 1811 in Franklin, Kentucky; Marriage 1 Mrs. Sarah Schmitt b: Abt 1830 in Louisiana. Married: After 1860 in (probably) Texas.[149]

48. Hitson, John and Bill (also spelled Hittson)—of Palo Pinto County, Stephenville, Texas.* They were Texas and Colorado cattle barons with a possible James family connection.

John Hittson's paternal uncle married Eliza Jane James.[150] He was once a partner of John Chisum, the famous New Mexico cattle baron who was identified with Billy the Kid.[151] Nathan Bedford Forrest was John Hittson's first cousin who became a three-star general in the Confederate Army and an early leader of the Ku Klux Klan (KKK).[152] It has been alleged that Nathan Bedford Forrest was one of the leaders of the Knights of the Golden Circle and Jesse James was their treasurer. The following article is written verbatim:

> John Nathan "Jack" Hittson was born 11 Oct 1831 in TN and died in an accident 25 Dec 1880 in Deer Trail, Colorado. He was one of the 2 sons of Jesse and Mary Ann Beck Hart. Hittson was the grandson of Alexander Eidson-Hittson, Boyse, and Edward Eidson. His father came to Texas in the 1840's to Rusk Co., and later moved to Pale Pinto County. He married Selena Frances Brown and fathered ten children.

---

*Correct names for the Hitson/Hittson brothers. According to the way my great-great-grandfather entered the names in his diary, it first appeared to read John Hitson and Bill Palopinto.

Between 1856 and 1874, John Nathan Hittson rose from a poor dirt farmer to become one of the wealthiest cattlemen in the U.S. Hittson and his close neighbors, Charles Goodnight, Oliver Loving, Marcus Dalton, C.C. Slaughter, and Kit Carter all became rich by discovering the earliest markets for longhorn cattle and prospering from the great beef market that exploded immediately after the Civil War.

Among his many achievements, "Cattle Jack" Hittson became sheriff of the tough and primitive Pale Pinto Co. in north-central TX. During the Civil War he served in the Confederate militia, survived numerous Indian battles, and nearly starved to death. After quitting the farm, he made several dangerous trips to the South, where he hauled salt and later drove cattle to Mexico. The meager profits from these trips caused him to become known as the richest man on the Texas Frontier. After assisting in the recovery of Cynthia Ann Parker from the Comanche's, he moved into Robert E. Lee's quarters at Camp Cooper and witnessed the destructive aftermath of the Kiowa Indian Chief Santana's attack on the Warren Wagon Train.

John Hittson gained fame when he hired a large, private army of gunmen and brazenly invaded New Mexico Terr. in search of Cattle-thieving Comancheros. Though he denied it, his gunmen killed several ranchers and townspeople who attempted to stop the Texas marauders. Ultimately, Hittson recovered $250,000 worth of stolen Texas cattle and horses. Aided by the U.S. Army, he was so powerful that he defied the territorial government and even advertised his exploits in the local New Mexican newspapers. From this frontier background he moved to gala parties among the highest social circles in Denver.[153]

Based on the fact that my great-great-grandfather had John and Bill Hittson's names and place of residence listed in his 1871–72 diary, it stands to reason that he may have been among the gunmen hired by them. Driving cattle through the streets of Denver with six-guns at his side and a Winchester "Yellow Boy" strapped to his saddle created the image of "Cattle Jack"—a man fully in charge of his destiny.[154]

Hittson remained a prominent stockman in Colorado until his death. Financial reverses associated with the panic of 1873, a lavish living style, and periodic problems with alcohol caused him to sell many of his cattle. At the time of his death, although he had far fewer than the estimated 100,000 head he possessed when in Texas, probate records for his estate indicate that he still had well over 20,000 head. On Christmas Day 1880 Hittson was killed when he was thrown from a wagon drawn by a runaway team of horses.[155]

He is buried in Hittson Cemetery.[156]

49. Hunt—My great-great-grandfather made the following diary entry on November 5, 1871: "Sunday morning at Miss Hunts and hunted cows all day and camped at Daises."

There were Hunts in Waco, McLennan County, Texas, who allegedly rode with the James-Younger Gang.[157] McLennan County adjoins Falls County, and the county line dividing them isn't far from Blevins where my great-great-grandfather lived. Waco is the county seat and is located about thirty miles north of Blevins, Texas. The following excerpt from a posting from the Hunt Family Genealogy Forum (written verbatim) relates that a Hunt who lived in Waco allegedly rode with the James-Younger Gang: "Looking for any info on my Grandpaw's kinfolk, he was from Waco, TX and said that one of his ancestors rode with the James Gang."[158]

A William Hunt from Missouri was in Collin County, Texas, in 1870:

"Hunt, William; Age; 30; White male; Born in Missouri but his Post Office was Farmersville, Collin County, Texas in 1870."[159]

Collin County joins Denton County on the east side and Dallas County on the north side. These counties are known to have been inhabited by ex-Quantrill Guerrillas after the Civil War.

According to author Carl Breihan, William Hunt did ride with Quantrill and Heritage Quest Online census records indicate that there was a William Hunt: "White male; Age: 19; Born in Kentucky but residing in Missouri, Clay County Fishing River Township in 1860 who may have been the William Hunt who rode with Quantrill."[160] He was the right age and lived in the same county in Missouri that Frank and Jesse James did.

On November 11, 1871, my great-great-grandfather made the following diary entry (written verbatim): "Saturday morning in camp on north elam and hunted down the creek all day and found 11 cows and then went across creek and pened for the night at Mrs. Hunt & William's hands were there." Was he referring to the William Hunt who rode with the James-Younger Gang?

Tom Hunt, a Quantrill guerrilla from Missouri, was once mistaken for Jesse James: "He was sentenced to three years in prison in Kentucky for being mistaken for Jesse James in the Mammoth Cave and Cave City stagecoach robbery on September 3, 1880. His trial was held on November 30, 1880, and he was bound over to the Barren County Grand Jury, which indicted him in April of 1881. The case came up for trial on March 31, 1882. He was found guilty and sentenced to three years in the penitentiary at Frankfurt, Kentucky. When Jesse James was killed in April of 1882, Hunt was given a full pardon on May 1, 1882. Ref: Block"[161]

50. Irvin—A Jesse James connection with variant spellings: Irvine, Irving, Irwin, Ervin, Erwine, Erwin.

J. C. Ervin rode with Quantrill. Most of the men who rode with Quantrill were from Missouri and were usually born from the mid- to late-1840s. A John Irvin who was born in Missouri in 1845 resided in Falls County, Texas, exactly where I believe Jesse James lived:

John Irvin; Age in 1870–24; Estimated Birth Year: 1845; Birthplace: Missouri; Home in 1870: Precinct 5, Falls, Texas; Race: White;

Gender: Male; Post Office: Carolina; Roll: M593_1584; Page:110; Image: 220; Year: 1870[162]

A William Irwin attended Quantrill reunions. Lankford writes that "J. C. Ervin attended several reunions (Quantrill) including the 1921 reunion. He was at the second burial of Jesse James in 1902."[163]

Or the Irvin my great-great-grandfather referred to may have been one of the following veterans who enlisted in Falls County, lived or were buried there post-Civil War, or belonged to the Falls Co. Willis L. Lang Camp of Confederate Veterans:

Erwin, Henry O., b. 1841, d. 1925, bur. Phillips Cem, Co K, 12 MS Cav

Irwin, George W., 1836, d. 1918, bur. P. Chapel Cem, Co C, 5 TX Inf (transfer from 34 MS Inf)

Irwin, W. H., b. -, d. -, bur. , Co B, 22 TX Inf, Travis, TX.[164]

51. Jackson—May have been Dan Jackson, Joe Jackson, J. Z. Jackson, or Terrell Jackson.

J. Z. Jackson was born February 28, 1847, died June 29, 1929, and is buried in Blevins Cemetery.[165] (My great-great-grandfather is also buried in Blevins Cemetery.) From the 1900 United States Federal Census:

Year: 1900; Census Place: Blevins, Falls, Texas; Roll: T623 1632; Page: 16B; Enumeration District: 28: Name: Joe Z Jackson; Home in 1900: Blevins, Falls, Texas; Age: 53; Estimated birth year: 1847; Birthplace: Georgia; Race: White; Relationship to head-of-house: Head; Spouse's name: H. A. Jackson; Father's birthplace: GA; Mother's birthplace: GA."

The following posting from Don Jackson on the Jackson Family Genealogy Forum reveals information about J. Z. Jackson: "Joseph

Z. Jackson born 2-28-1847 and died 1-17-1926 and is buried at the Cemetery at Blevins. He was a farmer at a community called Bell-Falls and was a 33rd degree Mason."[166] Bell Falls is located approximately three miles south of Blevins, Texas.

Another posting by Don reveals more information and relates that J. Z. Jackson wasn't a Civil War Veteran (or was he, but under a different name?). The following information is written verbatim:

> Joseph Zachariah Jackson was my great grandfather. He was born in Green Co. Georgia on Feb 28, 1847. He was the son of Floyd Jackson and Mary Fambrough Jackson. The Family moved to Texas in about 1856. Floyd was the foreman on the Hood plantation 10 miles south of Waco on the east side of the Brazos River. Floyd died in 1881 of the nosebleed.
>
> J. Z. was not a civil war veteran. He married Amanda Stevens in Blevins TX about 1870. Their children were Solomon, Aaron, Joseph Wooster (twin died at birth), Joel Wilson (twin my grandfather), and Mark. There were some daughters, one of which was Darrell I think. J. Z. died June 29, 1929 and Amanda died Jan.1926. J. Z. and Amanda are buried in the Blevins Cemetery in Falls Co. J. Z. was a 33rd degree Mason and taught Masonic work."[167]

Some claim that the 33 degree is the highest degree that can be reached by a Freemason. Many of Quantrill's men were Freemasons.

A bit of Civil War trivia: "While on their way to Texas, Jesse James, Dave Poole, and Press Webb broke a man named Jackson (a member of Shelby's brigade) out of jail."[168]

52. Jordan—May have been one of the Jordans living in Falls County, Texas, and listed below.

The following posting from the internet (written verbatim) reports that the Jordan Gang formed after the Civil War:

> The "Jordan Gang" was led by Benjamin F. Jordan, Captain of Confederate Home Guards. The Gang was made up of Confederate sympathizers in and around Pickens County, GA, which was mostly a pro-Union county during the War Between the States. Another such gang in this area was led by Benjamin F. McCollum. Both gangs increased their activity in 1864. This was after local northern sympathizers hung Benjamin's 75-year old father, Rev. Robert Jordan, because of his allegiance to the Confederacy. This was the same year that Sherman invaded Georgia.[169]

Some say that the Jordan Gang of outlaws was in league with "Bandit Queen" Belle Starr in the latter part of the 1800s.[170]

The following postings from the Jordan Family Genealogy Forum claim that a Jordan rode with Jesse James and that Jordans were related to him. The original post stated, "I am doing research on the Jordan's of MO for my friend. Her father mentioned that one of his ancestors rode with the James Gang but could not remember the name of this ancestor."[171] Another forum participant responded, "my Grandfather Ray Edward Jordan, who was born in 1899 in Coryell or Lampasas County, Texas used to tell his kids that his family was related to the James Gang, one of his family members was related to Jesse's Mom. Their ranch (Grandfather Jordan's) was outside Evant, (Coryell, County) Texas."[172]

53. Kinchelow—Probably Kincheloe. James Thomas Kincheloe rode with Quantrill during the Civil War (written verbatim):

> James Thomas Kincheloe served in the Confederate Army and rode with Quantrill for a short time. He was born in Morgan County, Missouri on February 22, 1864. James was the son of Lewis

Kincheloe who was a native of Ireland and mother, Mary Fountaine a native of France. The family came to Lafayette, Missouri in 1851. He married Jennie Taylor in Greentown, Missouri. He died near Higginsville, Missouri and is buried in Odessa Missouri Cemetery.[173]

James Kincheloe's family is known to have been in Texas after the Civil War. Census Records indicate that there was a James Kincheloe, a white male born in Missouri but living in Hill County, Texas, at the age of thirty-seven in 1880. Hill County is located just north of Waco, McLennan County, Texas. James Thomas Kincheloe's little brother, Massena F. Kincheloe, drowned in the Trinity River in Texas at an unspecified time. Some say he drowned near the close of the Civil War while others estimate his death as happening between 1848 and 1937. He was born in 1847 in Higginsville, Lafayette County, Missouri.[174] Although no information was given as to where on the Trinity River Massena Kincheloe drowned, it was probably in the Dallas/Denton/ Fort Worth area of Texas.

54. Maxey—My great-great-grandfather mentioned a Bill and Jim Maxey. The following excerpt relates an interesting story about the Maxi/Maxey name and Jesse James:

> After General Robert E. Lee's surrender at Appomattox, a force of 2,000 Missouri cavalry and a full regiment of Confederate-led Red Bone Indians from East Texas, led by General J. O. Shelby journeyed to Mexico to join their ally, the Emperor Maximilian. According to Schrader, Maximilian changed his name to John Maxi and began living undercover in North America. Jesse James traveled to Europe, found a double of Maximilian's wife, Carlotta, and then smuggled the real Carlotta back to America, where she was reunited with her husband. For their assistance, Maximilian rewarded the Knights of the Golden Circle $12.5 million in gold, and Jesse James $5 million.[175]

Bill Maxey may have been "William C. Maxey; Birth: 1854; Father: Newton Bennett Maxey; Mother: Susan Weathers. The Maxeys lived around the Lorena area of McLennan County, Texas."[176]

Jim Maxey was probably:

Jim G. Maxey; Birth: EST 1852; Marriage 1 Lucretta Barron b: 13 MAR 1861 in Waco, TX; Married: 26 JAN 1874 in Bell Co., TX; Divorced: yes.[177]

55. McDaniels, Tom—A Thompson "Tom" McDaniels rode with the James-Younger Gang.[178]

The James-Younger Gang is credited with robbing the West Virginia Bank of $10,000 on September 5, 1875, in Huntington, West Virginia.[179] James-Younger Gang member Tom McDaniel is claimed to have been killed by a farmer after this robbery . . . but was he?

On October 6, 1876, my great-great-grandfather entered in his diary that he saw Tom McDaniel on the road to Waco, Texas, and loaned him some money.

James-Younger Gang member Tom McDaniels is known to have been in Dallas, Texas, with the Younger brothers during the winter of 1870–71. Dallas is approximately one hundred miles north of Waco. "John Younger decided he was bored with the quiet life he was living in Missouri and made plans to return to the excitement offered by Dallas. The twenty-year-old renewed his employment at the dry goods store in the winter of 1870–71. With no one to supervise him, John then took up with some of the rowdier personalities, men whom Cole and Jim had advised him against. One of these, Tom McDaniels, the brother of one of Cole's guerrilla comrades, was in Texas under the alias of 'Tom Porter.'"[180]

According to *Branded as Rebels,* Tom McDaniels came from a well-respected family. The authors provide an excerpt from an article by the *Kansas City News-Chronicle:* "Thompson McDaniels was born in this city [Liberty] and is one of the three sons of

Thompson McDaniels, the builder of the Union Hotel and one of the best respected of the old citizens of Liberty. He is the oldest of the three sons. The youngest is now in Kansas, a steady hard-working man. His brother, Bud, was shot in the attempt to escape from the Lawrence jail. Since the death of his brother Bud, Thompson has not been seen in this vicinity. From the description, family and friends deny that the dead robber is Thompson McDaniels. Some think the dead man was Jesse James."[181]

One can't always rely on information that members of the James-Younger Gang or Quantrill men were killed as history reports. The Tom McDaniel my great-great-grandfather saw on the road to Waco was probably the same Tom McDaniel who rode with Jesse James.

Tom McDaniel's family and friends denied that he was killed in Huntington, Virginia.[182] But one news article claims that he was definitely killed (written verbatim):

Tom McDaniels was reported killed by the Sedalia Daily Democrat—Sedalia, Missouri—9/23/1875: Mystery Cleared up-Identification of Dead Virginia Bank Robber; He Is the Notorious Thompson McDaniels. A correspondent of the St. Louis Times of yesterday thus telegraphs from Pine Hill, Kentucky, in regard to the dead robber recognized as one of the Huntington, VA bank robbers: When I went into the house the body had been laid out decently for the grave. There were other visitors at the same time, and I confess my nerves had been wrought so that there was a slight tremor. The sheet was drawn down, and as I expected the features bore no likeness to those of Jesse James, whose face years ago were as familiar to me as the face of a daily acquaintance. There came an unexpected shock, however, for like a flash I recognized the face of Thompson McDaniels, a desperado known to thousands of people in Western Missouri. Thompson McDaniels has not been in the papers much but he has a terribly desperate record of (illegible) in Western Missouri. He was a bushwhacker of the worse type during the war, and the brother of Bud or Bill McDaniels, who was killed in Kansas not long since. Thompson has been virtually an outlaw nearly ten years. In 1867 he was arrested in Lafayette County, Missouri, for taking horses, but got off for turning state's evidence and betraying his partners. Sometime after that, he shot without provocation an old man named Seth Mason, and only escaped lynching by fleeing from Missouri. He spent some time in Texas where he will be remembered as the slayer of Colonel Nicholas, and ex-Confederate officer of Shelby's famous brigade.

Bill McDaniel's will be readily remembered by your readers as one of the five who robbed the Kansas Pacific Train at Muncie on the eighth of last December and plundered the express car of thirty thousand dollars in greenbacks and gold dust. Within a few days after the robbery, he ventured back to Kansas City, where he lived and had been arrested on a trivial charge and was found to have on him some of the plunder. He was indicted for the robbery, and, it is said, in a partial confession implicated his brother Thompson McDaniel in the robbery, with three other desperados, who had come up from their lurking places in the Indian Nation especially to do this job.[183]

56. McPhearson—McPhersons are buried in Blevins Cemetery along with my great-great-grandfather. Joe McPherson was said to have been doing some yard work for my great-great-grandfather and found some of his buried gold. The story goes that he was afraid to tell my great-great-grandfather about it because he was afraid that he would think he was trying to steal it. (George Roming and Doris Spidel related that story. Both were raised in Blevins near my great-great grandfather's farm and personally knew him.) One website states, "Joe Davis McPhearson, 1899–1985, husband of Beulah Huber McPherson; son of John F. & Alice McPherson; brother of Nora McPherson & Ollie Franklin."[184]

57. Mill___, (Illegible) George (George Miller?)—A possible Jesse James connection. A George Miller is said to have been the cousin of known James-Younger Gang member Clell Miller. "Moses Miller, Clell's father, had a brother Tobias Miller who lived in Daviess County, Missouri. His son was George W. Miller. He was in the Confederate Army and after the war came home to Missouri and then moved to Texas. He would have been older than Clell but a cousin to him. "[185]

A George Miller who was born in Missouri lived in Milam County, Texas, in 1870. Milam County adjoins Falls County. An ancestry.com search yielded the following:

> Name: Geo Miller; Age in 1870: 21; Estimated Birth Year: 1848; Birthplace: Missouri; Home in 1870: Not Stated, Milam, Texas; Race: White; Gender: Male; Post Office: Cameron; Roll: M593_1598 Page: 274; Image: 544; Year: 1870.

58. Moore, John—A possible Jesse James connection. Rosemary Lankford, author of *The Encyclopedia of Quantrill's Guerrillas*, reports that a John Moore rode with Jesse James after the Civil War. She writes:

> John Moore may have lived near Mrs. Fristoe, the grandmother of Cole Younger. His wife was Josephine. He was the son-in-law of David Yeager. In the 1860 Missouri census, Cornelius Moore was 28 years old. His wife was Josephine. This may be John Moore. In May of 1862, Jarrette and Younger were at his home waiting for word from Quantrill. He was wounded near Fred Farmer's home. One source listed Moore as a member of the James Gang, and that Moore went to Kentucky and died there.[186]
>
> The 1860 Federal Census records for Clay County, Missouri, list a John Moore: Moore, John; State: MO; Year: 1860; County: Clay County; Record Type: Federal Population Schedule; Township: Platte Township.[187]

Or the John Moore my great-great-grandfather referred to may have been the son of the Robert Moore who came to Falls County, Texas, from South Carolina:

Robert was born 1812 in Ireland, died September 1880 at Mooreville, Falls County, Texas and buried there.

Among the six children of Robert M. and Marguerite (Wiley) Moore were sons, John Thomas Moore—b 1841 in Mississippi, d March 1901 at Eddy, Texas, married Jane ("Jenny") Williams— and Robert D. Moore—b March 10, 1849 in Washington County, Texas, died at Bruceville, Texas. The village that developed where Robert Moore lived was named Mooreville in his honor.[188]

59. Moore, Robert—A Robert Moore rode with Quantrill.[189] Lankford describes who this may be. "In the 1860 Missouri census, Jackson County, Fishing River, R. M. Moore (who may have been the Robert Moore that rode with Quantrill), a 27 year old farmer, was born in Ohio. His wife, Mary A., a 23 year old Indian, was born in Kansas Territory."[190]

From the Missouri Census, 1830–70:

Moore, Robert; State: MO; Year: 1860; County: Clay County; Record Type: Federal Population Schedule; Township: Fishing River Township; Page: 854; Database: MO 1860 Federal Census Index.[191]

Or Robert Moore may have been the brother of the John Moore listed above who lived in Falls County, Texas, in 1870. There is always the possibility that the John and Robert Moore connected to Jesse James and Quantrill were the same John and Robert Moore living in Falls County, Texas.

60. Mrs. Nolens (Nolan/Noland?)—May have been "Emma Nolan; Age 38; White female; Born in North Carolina but was living in Falls County, Texas in 1870."[192]

There were at least eight Nolans/Nolands who rode with Quantrill: Edward, George M., George W., Henry, James, John, Morgan, Thomas, and William.[193]

61. Pickit, Cournal (Colonel)—Lived four miles northeast of Decatur, Texas. An online source describes him as follows:

> George B. Pickett, rancher, soldier, politician. . . . At the age of ten he traveled to Clarksville, Red River County, Texas, with his family. . . . In August 1854 he traveled southwest from Clarksville through Denton County into central Wise County. Attracted by abundant pastureland, he purchased the claim of Jim Rogers, four miles north of Decatur. Later he moved his home site a mile southeast to be near the banks of Catlett Creek.
>
> Shortly after Texas voted in favor of secession, Pickett raised a company of 100 men and was elected captain of Company B, Fifteenth Texas Cavalry. In March 1862 he was promoted to major. When the regiment was reorganized at Little Rock, Arkansas, Pickett was promoted to lieutenant colonel. . . . A week before Gen. Robert E. Lee surrendered, Throckmorton ordered Pickett to find and return a band of 100 deserters from the Confederate Army who were attempting to escape into New Mexico. Pickett captured the soldiers and returned them to face trial for desertion. This action produced numerous threats on Pickett's life from angry citizens in and around the county. But with the war's end and the remembrance of Pickett's reputation as one of the leading citizens of the county, the anger subsided and was soon forgotten.
>
> By 1870 Pickett was one of the prominent stockmen in North Texas. He ran cattle on land near Decatur in Wise County, as well as on rangeland in Jack and Young counties. . . . Pickett was elected to the first of five terms as a member of the Texas House of representatives in 1874. . . . Between 1876 and 1878 he served

as county judge. He returned to the legislature in the early 1880s for three more terms as representative.[194]

62. Powers, John—A Texas cattleman who knew Allen Parmer (Frank and Jesse James's brother-in-law). He married Nancy Caroline Barron, daughter of Thomas Hudson Barron and Barron's first wife Mary Elizabeth Robinson Carnall. According to one online post:

John W. M. Powers, Birth: 29 Oct 1847 (some sources say 1848) in Wilderville, Falls, TX; Death: 10 Aug 1886 in Wilderville, Falls, TX. "John Sr. went on cattle drives to Kansas and possibly died from an accidental fall from a hotel window in Kansas City, Missouri."

Father: Lewis Barker Powers b: 31 May 1820 in TN; Mother: Nancy Caroline Barron b: 13 Oct 1827 in Little Rock, Phillips, Arkansas; *Marriage* 1 Susan Roberts in May 1868, Wilderville, Falls County, Texas. Children: James H. Powers b: 15 Apr 1869; and John W. M. Powers Jr. b: 5 Jun 1870.[195]

As stated earlier John Powers knew Allen Parmer, Frank and Jesse James's brother-in-law (written verbatim):

In 1880, John Powers established his headquarters at Jaybuckle Springs with the "Jaybuckle" brand. It was located at the crossing of Elm Creek due North of the present town of Reed. Samuel Houston Tittle was his foreman until 1887. Powers was joined by Handy and Haney, who ran the "H-Bar-Y" brand. In 1885 the Haney's sold to "Doc Day."

A gate, through which the early settlers came to Mangum, was located near the dugout home of the late W. J. Reeves, father of Lige Reeves. Doan's Crossing was the Gateway to old Greer County, Texas and Corwin T. Doan sat in his sod trading post and saw the trail driver, the ranchman, and the settlers come into Greer County. Alan Farmer (Parmer), brother-in-law of outlaws Frank and Jessie

James, ran cattle in the 80's around the mouth of Station Creek (in Northeast Greer County, Texas.) Farmer (Parmer) was a frequent visitor to the County while his cattle were on the range but he never lived in the County nor brought his family to Greer County, Texas.[196]

John W. Powers also helped establish the Day Land and Cattle Company, "a private corporation with headquarters in Austin, was organized on March 24, 1884, by James Monroe Day, Charles E. Anderson, Frank M. Maddox, John W. Maddox, and John W. Powers to buy, sell, and lease Texas land for grazing and breeding beef cattle. The company, chartered for fifty years with a capital stock of $510,000, bought 174,854 acres of donation and bounty land scrip and leased several thousand acres. On August 4, 1885, it leased 203,000 acres in Greer County. The loss of this property to Oklahoma was probably at least partly responsible for the firm's decline."[197]

63. Reed—A possible Jesse James connection. The Reed Family Genealogy Forum provided an interesting story about a connection to James "Jim" Reed—Belle Starr's first husband who rode with Quantrill—and Wise County, Texas:*

As you are probably aware, Jesse James' sister lived in Wichita Falls and is buried in Riverside Cemetery there. The only tie to the Reeds I know of is that the James boys and James C. Reed (first and legal husband of Myra Maybelle Shirley a.k.a. Belle Starr) rode with Quantrill during the Civil War. Jim Reed was the son of Solomon Reed and Susan Brock of Vernon Co., MO. Also, Jim's grandparents (the Perry Green Brocks) and Aunt Fatima Brock and her husband David Reed (cousin to Jim Reed's father) lived in Cass Co., MO prior

---

*My great-great-grandfather purchased his 1871–72 diary in Wise County, Texas, and knew people there.

to 1860. When the Brocks and David Reeds moved to Wise Co., TX Cole Younger's uncle purchased the David Reed farm in MO.[198]

64. Reed, William (Reid)—Most sources claim that the William Reed/Reid who married Serena Barron was born in Louisiana on October 18, 1852, and served the Confederacy in Louisiana:

> William J. Reid: 18 OCT 1852 in Louisiana; Death: 26 FEB 1925 in Loco, OK; Marriage 1 Serena Barron b: 23 June 1856 in Waco, TX; Married: 25 JAN 1872 in Falls Co. TX.
> Serena E Barron, born July 23, 1856 in Blevins or Waco, TX; died 3/07/1933 in Alma, OK; married (1) William Jonah Reid 1/25/1872 in Falls Co, TX; married (2) James Losson Quinn April 22, 1902.

Ancestry.com reports the following information:

> Private Reid William J.; Company G; Unit 17 Louisiana Infantry; Allegiance: Confederate.

Was this the William Reed who married Serena Barron? Simple math indicates that the William J. Reed born on October 18, 1852, is highly unlikely to have been the William J. Reid who was a Confederate soldier listed above. According to this William Reid's date of birth, October 18, 1852, he would have only been nine years old when the Civil War officially began on April 12, 1861, and by the time the War ended in 1865, he would have been about thirteen.

There are accounts of boys of that age serving in the Civil War in some capacity, but the average age for soldiers of the regular Confederate and Union Armies was eighteen. If they were younger than that a parent or legal guardian was usually required to give their written permission.[199]

Or the Reed my great-great-grandfather referred to may have been:

> William H. Read, born 1837, d. -, bur. -, Co B, 5 TX Cav., was a veteran who enlisted in Falls Co; lived or was buried there

post-Civil War; or belonged to the Falls Co Willis L. Lang Camp of Confederate Veterans.[200]

65. Scott, Bill—A W. W. Scott lived in Bell County, Texas. Bell County adjoins Falls County, which is where my great-great-grandfather lived. In fact, he lived very near the boundary line dividing the two counties. Online census records tell of:

William "Bill" W. Scott; White male; Age 41; Born in Missouri but lived in Bell County, Texas in 1880. Bessie A. Scott, wife of a W. W. Scott, is buried in Blevins Cemetery, Blevins, Texas.[201]

A W. W. Scott was a boyhood friend of Quantrill. An article in *American Heritage* magazine shares the following:

In 1887 William W. Scott, a boyhood friend of Quantrill, traveled to Kentucky, opened his grave, and took the remains back to Dover for reburial. Not all of the skeleton went into the ground, however. Scott secretly retained the skull and at least five bones. After his death the skull "disappeared," only to resurface in 1972, when it was donated to the Dover Historical Society. The director sent it to the anthropology department at Kent State University, where a wax head and face were constructed, using the skull as a model, complete with glass eyes and a wig.[202]

66. Singleton, Bud—Bud Singleton rode with the James-Younger Gang.[203] Given the fact that there are other names listed in my great-great-grandfather's diary that also match known members of the James-Younger Gang, I have no doubt that this Bud Singleton was the same Bud Singleton who rode with Jesse James.

Bud Singleton was probably one of the sons of Colonel Middleton Glaize Singleton, an officer in the Confederate Army living in Boone County, Missouri, at the time of Quantrill's Lawrence Raid.[204]

On the night of September 26, 1863, Jesse James was camped on the Singleton farm near Booneville, Missouri, with hundreds of other guerrillas under Quantrill who were preparing to ride into Lawrence, Kansas the next morning. Stiles describes the scene this way:

To Jesse James, the sprawling camp on Young's Creek was a rare sight. Only once before (with Thornton in Platte County) had the seventeen-year-old wandered among so many campfires, so many horses unsaddled, so many boots being shaken out, so many blankets and socks hanging out to dry. Some two hundred to four hundred guerrillas spread out on the property of Colonel M. G. Singleton, a Confederate officer now living at home on parole.[205]

Genealogical information about Middleton Glaize Singleton lists

Middleton Glaize Singleton; Title: Col.; Birth: 15 SEP 1821 in St. Landry Parish, Louisiana; Death: 13 JUN 1893; Burial: Columbia Cemetery, Boone County, Missouri. . . .
   Marriage 2 Mary Eliza Barr b: 19 FEB 1829 in Missouri
   Married: 23 SEP 1847 in Boone County, Missouri
   Children: Charles G. Singleton b: ABT. 1849 in Missouri; Robert B. Singleton b: ABT. 1851 in Missouri; Seth Singleton b: ABT. 1854 in Missouri; Clinton Singleton b: ABT. 1858 in Missouri; and Middleton G. Singleton, Jr. b: 1859 in Missouri.[206]

Bud may have been a nickname for Charles G. Singleton or his brother, Robert B. Singleton. Charles was the right age to have served in the Civil War (I have noticed that most of Quantrill's men were born in the mid-1840s.), supporting the theory that Bud Singleton was from the Singleton family listed above.

67. Stone—According to George Roming, a former resident of Blevins, Texas, a Stone living in the Blevins area rode with Quantrill before coming to Blevins.

There are fifteen Stones listed in Joanne Eakin and Donald Hale's *Branded as Rebels*. A William Stone rode with Jesse James during the Civil War. "At least five of the Stones listed attended Quantrill Reunions: Stone, G. T.; Stone, Lee; Stone, P. L.; Stone, Sam; Stone, Thomas B; Stone, survived War At Fayette 20 Sept 1864, wounded."[207]

The Stone my great-great-grandfather referred to may have been one of the following Stones who were veterans who enlisted in Falls Co; lived or were buried there post-Civil War; or belonged to the Falls Co Willis L. Lang Camp of Confederate Veterans:

Stone, B. M., b. -, d. bur. -, Sgt, Co E, 6 TX Cav, Gatesville, TX
Stone, W., b. 1846, d. 1944, bur. P. Chapel Cem, Co E, 2 MS Cav.[208]

68. Vestal—A Vestal was a good friend of Frank and Jesse James (written verbatim):

The Joab Vestal family, with connections to the James L Courtney story, moved from Arkansas with final destination in Lamar County, Texas. Joab Vestal Sophronia Spencer. This Vestal family of Texas can be traced back to the David Vestal who is said to have been born in 1821 and died in 1863 in Buchanan, Missouri.

Trailing the Vestal family from Missouri to Arkansas and then Texas takes us to them living in Leon County, Marques, Texas, Falls County, Rusk, Limestone, Grosebeck, Palmer, Parker County, Ellis County, and Hardeman County. Joab and his family can be found on the census records pg 119 b 1870 Falls County, Texas Census records: pg 168 West of the Brazos 22 Sep 1870 McLennan County, Texas. From this same family is Charles R Vestal who was a good friend of Frank and Jesse James.

Charles R. VESTAL Born: JUN 1872 in Palmer, Ellis Co., Texas Death: MAY 1933 in Hardeman Co., Texas: *Fact 1:* 1920 Superintendent at Cement Mill; *Fact 2:* 1900 moved from

Ellis Co. TX to Hardeman Co. TX; *Fact 3:* ABT. 1895 was a friend of outlaw Frank James.

Permelia Vestal, daughter of Joab and Sophronia Spencer, married Harris D Record. She married second to John Densman of Missouri. John was the son of Thomas R Densman born 1792 in Pa and died 1868 in Benton, Missouri. His mother was Nancy Yarnell born 1807 in Howard County, Missouri. Thomas Densman, father of John Densman, was a farmer in Missouri.[209]

69. Vestal, David—I found no genealogical information for him but *Branded as Rebels* lists him as a bushwhacker: "David Vestal was a bushwhacker that is claimed to have been killed Arnoldsville and Agency Ford, Buchanan County, Missouri."[210]

The key phrase in the sentence above is "claimed to have been killed." Did David Vestal die as reported, or did he do just as numerous other known bushwhackers, Confederate guerrillas, and James-Younger Gang members did and fake his death? Is he the same David Vestal who was in Falls County, Texas, with my great-great-grandfather?

I find it intriguing that federal census records for Buchanan County, Missouri (listed below), indicate that a David Vestal had a John and James White living in his household while *Branded as Rebels* reports the following: "James White was suspected as being in the robbery of the bank at Savannah, Missouri on March 2, 1867. John White was supposed to have been with Jesse James after the war."[211]

The census record states:

State: Missouri; Year: 1860; County: Buchanan County; Record Type: Federal Population Schedule; Township: Jackson Township: Vestal, David; Age 39; White male; Farmer; Born in North Carolina; Vestal, Jane; Age 33, White female, Born in Missouri; Vestal, Martha A., Age 16, White female, Born in Missouri; Vestal, Mary F., Age 13, White female, Born in Missouri; Vestal, Sarah B. , Age 11 White female, Bin Missouri; Vestal, Harriet C.,

Age 8, White female, Born in Missouri; Vestal, James A.; Age 2; White male; Born in Missouri; White, John; Age 21, White male, Farmhand; Born in Ireland; and White, James; Age 18; White male; Farmhand; Born in Ireland.[212]

I find it equally intriguing that a David Vestal came to see my great-great-grandfather on November 23, 1871: "Thirsday morning at Mr. Barron's & remained at the house all day and do nothing & David Vestal came here in the evening."

The fact that my great-great-grandfather also mentions a J. White in his diary only adds to the intrigue. Was the bushwhacker David Vestal the same David Vestal who lived in Jackson, Missouri, in 1860 and allegedly died there in 1863? Were the James and John White who lived with him the suspected James-Younger Gang members? Were they the men with identical names mentioned in my great-great-grandfather's diary?

Besides other men with names identical to known James-Younger Gang members mentioned in my great-great-grandfather's diary, other Vestals born in North Carolina with Missouri connections were also mentioned.

70. Waggoner, Dan—A Jesse James connection.

Dan Waggoner was a legend in his own time and is to this day. He epitomizes the legendary wealthy Texan rancher/oil tycoon. He named one of his famous Waggoner Ranch Quarter Horses "Jesse James."[213] For Waggoner to have named one of his famous horses Jesse James, he must have regarded him highly and according to the information below he apparently knew him personally.

Dan Waggoner lived in Wise County, Texas (recall that my great-great-grandfather purchased his 1871 diary there).

The Texas Handbook Online describes Allison, Texas, where the Waggoners lived, as "a farm community on a spur of U.S. Highway 380 two miles west of the Denton county line in eastern Wise County. The site was originally owned by cattleman Daniel Waggoner and his son William Thomas Waggoner. In the 1870s outlaws Jesse and Frank James and Texas bandit Sam Bass hid from the law near the site."[214]

Dan Waggoner's name and city of residence are among those listed in Jesse's diary. T. J. Waggoner, nephew of Dan Waggoner, reminisces about meeting Frank and Jesse James in Texas:

I was born May 22, 1861 in a log cabin on a farm about three miles east of Decatur, in Wise County, Texas. I was the oldest boy and the second oldest of seven children. My father's name was John Waggoner. He was born in Missouri and came to Texas with his family when a young boy, and the family settled in Hopkins County. My father and his brother Dan married sisters in Hopkins County. Their maiden name was Moore. After my father and Dan married they left the rest of the folks and came to Wise County. They started raising cattle and farming. This was about 1852. When the war broke out my Father went to war, but his brother stayed at home. . . .

One time in 1879 . . . I spent the night with Allen Parmer who lived down Wichita River east of our headquarters. Two men came in late and ate supper and we sat around and talked. The next morning when I ate breakfast with the family I was informed that the two men had left before I got up. I don't remember what name they were introduced to me by, but anyhow it did not make any impression. Several years later I met Frank James at John Fore's Livery stable here in Wichita Falls, and he asked me about this night I stayed with Allen Parmer, and he said that he and his brother Jesse were the two men that I had met that night. He and Jesse were brothers of Allen Parmer's wife, and they would sometimes come down here to lay low after committing some crimes back in Missouri or the Territory."[215]

A cowhand, McGuire, who worked for the Waggoner Ranch, also told the following story. It rings true because my great-great-grandfather was in Texas in the early 1870s.

With an Irish accent, an Irish chuckle, and an Irish twinkle in his eye, James McGuire, 98-year-old veteran of the Civil War, is an interesting talker. He visits his son G. R. McGuire in Wichita Falls, Texas. Though at present (1937) a resident of the Soldier's Home in Leavenworth, Kansas, Wichita Falls claims him as he was a cowhand for Waggoner in the early days.

[He said] "One of the most daring escapes made by Jesse and Frank James was a $80,000 bank robbery at Clarkville, Texas, on the Red River, in the early 70s. Jesse swung into the town on a horse back one day and single handed took that amount. Officers, giving pursuit shot the horse from under him. He met his brother Frank on the other side of the river."[216]

Census information for Daniel Waggoner follows:

Daniel "Dan" Waggoner; Birth: 7 JUL 1828 1 2 3 4 in Lincoln County, Tennessee; Death: 5 SEP 1902 1 3 4 in Colorado; Burial: Oaklawn Cemetery, Decatur, Wise County, Texas; Description: tall and blue-eyed; Residence: AFT 1840 1 Hopkins County, Texas; Residence: Cactus Hill 1851 1 18 miles west of Decatur, Wise County, Texas; PROP: 15,000 acres in 1850 Denton Creek, Wise County, Texas; PROP: property AFT 1870 1 Wilbarger, Foard, Wichita, Baylor, Archer, and Knox Counties, Texas.

The Handbook of Texas Online describes the family's history as follows:

The Waggoner (Three D) Ranch had its beginnings in the early 1850s when Daniel Waggoner and a fifteen-year-old black slave trailed 242 longhorn cattle and six horses into Wise County. Waggoner first settled his wife and son, William Thomas (Tom) Waggoner, in a home on Catlett Creek near the site of present Decatur. Two years later, after buying an additional 200 head,

Waggoner located his herd on a 15,000-acre tract on the West Fork of the Trinity River near Cactus Hill, in the vicinity of present Lake Bridgeport. However, because of the increasing danger of Indian raids, he was compelled to move his family back to Denton Creek temporarily. His first brand was a D61, but about 1866 he began branding with three Ds in reverse, a brand easy to recognize and difficult for rustlers to alter. He used a D71 brand on his horses until around 1881. By 1869 Dan and Tom Waggoner had formed a partnership known as D. Waggoner and Son. Late that year they wintered a herd in Clay County and in the spring of 1870 drove it to the Kansas market, netting a profit of $55,000, which was the basis of their ranch fortune. In 1871, with the westward push of the frontier, the Waggoners moved their headquarters to Clay County, settling temporarily on the Wichita River in southeastern Wichita County. From that site they moved the headquarters to the junction of China Creek and the Red River in northwestern Wichita County, just north of what is now Electra, which was named for Tom's daughter. By the early 1880s their range extended thirty miles from China Creek to Pease River. In 1885 the need for more grassland prompted them to lease 650,000 acres of range land in the 'Big Pasture,' part of the Comanche and Kiowa reservation lands across the Red River in Indian Territory. With the passing of the open range they began purchasing Texas land. Paying about $1 an acre, the Waggoners slowly built their cattle and horse empire. Between 1889 and 1903 the ranch came to cover a block running thirty miles east and west and twenty-five miles north and south, including more than a million acres. It extended into Foard, Knox, Baylor, and Archer counties but centered chiefly in Wilbarger and Wichita counties. . . .

Dan Waggoner died in September 1904. In 1909 Tom Waggoner divided half of the ranch among his three children, Paul, Guy, and Electra, as a Christmas gift mainly to give them training in ranching. The discovery of oil at Electra in 1911 caused the Waggoners to combine oil production and refining with ranching activities; the refinery cars and tanks bore the image of the Waggoner cattle brand.[217]

71. Walker, J.—Lived in Clifton, Bosque County, Texas. May have been the Andrew J. Walker who rode with Quantrill.

In the "Summary of John Walker, A Supplement of the Riley Walker and His Family," written by Glenn Walker (now deceased), there is the following: "Glenn was a great-grandson of John Walker & Talitha Tipton Walker. In this book it states that Andrew J. Walker rode with both Wm. Quantrill and the James Gang. Jesse and Frank James both rode with Quantrill."[218]

An online post shares the following:

Andrew J. Walker saved Quantrill's life on two occasions. Leaving Price's Army Quantrill informed Andrew of a plan to raid the home of Andrew's father, Morgan. Informed neighbors, probably because of his attraction to Walker's sister, Nannie (Anna) and with eleven others defeated the marauders. She became Quantrill's mistress. In this action, the first Union soldier killed in Jackson County during the Civil War was killed by Quantrill. She was later won over by Joe Vaughan. This was the first mention of Quantrill's named in Jackson County, Mo.[219]

Andrew Walker is described by Edward E. Leslie in the book *The Devil Knows How to Ride* as a modest man who stood up for Quantrill numerous times, preventing his lynching as described by the following: "A great many people were in town the next day and the excitement ran very high. In the afternoon I thought it time to start home and went to the stable to get my horse. When I arrived on the public square, I found a great crowd gathered about. I rode up to them to see what it meant and learned that they were going to hang Quantrill. . . . I told them they must not do it; but some of them seemed inclined to be stubborn about it. I told them if they did, they would do it over my dead body and they gave it up."[220]

The J. Walker my great-great-grandfather referred to lived in Bosque County, Texas. Andrew J. Walker who rode with Quantrill is known to have lived in Weatherford, Parker County, Texas. Parker County is separated from Bosque County by Hood County. More than likely the J. Walker my great-great-grandfather referred to was the Andrew J. Walker who rode with Quantrill.

72. Whatley—A Jesse James connection. The following information was written by genealogist/historian Carol Holmes, and is presented verbatim:

Little would anyone suspect that the Whatley family of Falls County is connected to the same Woodson family of Jesse Woodson James. I'll begin with Mary Caroline Whatley. Mary was born May 1, 1847 in Georgia. She died March 14, 1895 and is buried in Blevins Cemetery, Falls Co., TX. What makes her so interesting is that she married John Wesley STANDRIDGE of Alabama. John fought in the Confederate Army in the Civil War, Company K 1st Texas Infantry. [Lou Kilgore, a genealogist and James family historian, is related to this Standridge family.] Mary Caroline Whatley is the daughter of Wilson Whatley and Mary Hanson. Her brother, Calvin L Whatley, married Mary Elizabeth "Jane" Kilgore.

After their marriage Wilson and Mary lived in the twenty ninth District of Fayette County, Georgia until about 1858 when they immigrated to Texas. They settled near the farm of Henry Duty and Fielden Ruble on the West Side of the Brazos River. Wilson worked for Henry Duty, on his farm in Falls County, Texas. The 1860 Census indicated that seven children, born in Georgia, came with them and they had one more in Falls County. Their descendants said that they had eight of twelve children to survive.

There have been descendants of Wilson and Mary Whatley

in Falls County for over 125 years. Where the Woodson family ties into the Whatley family takes place with the son of Ornan Bradley Whatley Sr. and Judith Thornton. Wilson Whatley married first to Tabitha Wheelwright. He married second to Sarah Heard. Sarah Heard is the daughter of Thomas Heard Sr. and Elizabeth Napier Fitzpatrick. Elizabeth Napier Fitzpatrick is the daughter of Joseph Fitzpatrick and Mary Perrin Woodson. Mary Perrin Woodson is the daughter of Benjamin Woodson and Francis Napier. Benjamin Woodson is the son of John Woodson Jr. and Mary Tucker. John Woodson Jr. is the son of John Woodson Sr. wife unknown. John Woodson Jr's brother Robert Woodson married Elizabeth Farris.

John Woodson who married Mary Tucker had a son Benjamin Woodson who married Francis Napier. His father John Woodson 1655 in Curles, Henrico Co. Sarah Mary Pleasant. John Woodson b. 1655 was the son of Dr. John Woodson born 1586 in Dorchester, Devonshire, England. Dr. John Woodson graduated from St. John's College, Bristol, England in 1604. He married Sarah Winston.

John and Sarah left for America on the ship George on 29 Jan 1619 and arrived in Jamestown, Virginia on April 1619. Remember Jamestown was founded in 1607 and Mass., Bay Colony 1620 (Pilgrims F/Mayflower). John was employed as a surgeon for a company of soldiers sent over for protection of the colony from Indians. Sir George Yeardly, the first Governor of Virginia and his wife, Temperance Flowerdew, were also aboard the ship which totaled 100 passengers. John and Sarah located at Flowerdew Hundred (a.k.a. Fleur de Hundred, Four De Hundred and Piesery's Hundred), which was on the south side of the James River, located about 30 miles above Jamestown, in what is now Prince George County. John and Sarah had two sons, John Jr. (born 1632) and Robert (born 1634). In 1632, Dr. Woodson was listed as Surgeon of the Flour De Hundred Colony. On 18 April 1644, he was returning from visiting a patient and was killed by Indians in sight of his home. The Indians then attached [attacked] the house, which was barred against them and defended by his wife, Sarah, and a man named Thomas Ligon (a shoemaker). The only weapon they had was an old time gun (8 ft. long with a 1" diam, bor), which Ligon handled with deadly effect. At the first fire he killed 3 Indians, and two at the second shot. In the meantime, 2 Indians came down the chimney, but Sarah scalded one to death with a pot of boiling water which stood on the fire. Then, seizing the iron roasting spit with both hands, she brained the other Indian, killing him instantly. The howling mob on the outside took fright and fled, but Ligon fired the 3rd time and killed two more, making 9 dead in all.

At the first alarm, Sarah had hidden her two boys, one under a large washtub and the other in a hole where they kept potatoes during the winter. This was done hoping to save the boys in the event the Indians succeeded in entering the rude log cabin in which they lived. For several generations, the descendants of one of these boys was called "Tub Woodson" and the other "Potato Hole (or Tater-hoe) Woodson." If you ever come across another Woodson descendant, the first thing they'll probably ask is Tub or Tater-hole. Your response Sharlee [surely] should be Tater-hole, for we're all descended from Robert Woodson and his wife, Elizabeth Ferris.

Dr. John Woodson son Robert, Col. Woodson is the seed line of Jesse James. Col. Robert Woodson married Elizabeth Ferris. Their son Benjamin Woodson, not to be confused with the Benjamin Woodson of our sketch, married Sarah Porter. Their son Robert Woodson III married Rebecca Pryor. Their daughter Elizabeth Woodson married Shadrick Mimms. Their daughte Elizabeth Mimms would marry Robert Poor. Their daughter Mary Polly Poor married John M James and they were the parents of Robert Sallee James and grandparents of Frank and Jesse James. So in a little town called Blevins, Texas hidden among names of forgotten past lived the seed line of Jesse James starting with a little hidden mystery of the Whatley family.[221]

73. White, J.—A possible James-Younger Gang connection. Given the number of other men listed in my great-great-grandfather's diary who rode with Quantrill and later Jesse James, J. White could have been the James or John White who rode with Jesse.

The following J. Whites are listed in *Branded as Rebels*:
- Josiah White rode with Quantrill.
- James White was a suspect in the Liberty and Richmond bank robberies in Missouri. He was arrested at St. Joseph on suspicion of the Liberty robbery but released. Later, he was accused of robbing the Independence bank. Although he was a suspect in the Savannah robbery, he was not arrested. He robbed the Russellville bank, and was accused of the Corydon (Iowa) bank robbery. A $5,000 reward for his arrest was placed over his head. He left for Kentucky.
- John White lived in Texas for a while, and then went to Mexico and died there.[222]

One source states that the White family helped Frank and Jesse James (written verbatim): "Robert E. White b. 07/25/1864 in MO is my ggrandfather. The story that he told me when I was a child was that when he was a young boy in MO, Frank and Jesse James were on the run from the law and his family gave shelter to the James gang since his family was 'Southern sympathizers'. He also told me that his father was for the South while his uncle was for the North. Robert White's family left MO around 1878-1880 and settled in Hood County, TX (near Ft. Worth, TX)."

The following posting from the White Family Genealogy Forum on the internet relates that the White family was related by marriage to Frank and Jesse James through their stepfather, Dr. Reuben Samuel (written verbatim):

According to my info, Mary White Samuel was the step-grandmother of Jessie and Frank James. Mary White Samuel was married to Fielding Samuel in Kentucky and they were the parents of Dr. Rueben Samuel. After the death of two husbands, Zerelda James (mother of Frank and Jesse) married Dr. Rueben Samuel. Fielding and Mary White Samuel appear on the 1850 Missouri census as the family apparently moved from Kentucky to Missouri between 1848 and 1850. Fielding and Mary left Missouri around 1875 and settled near Clifty community in Northwest Arkansas to avoid constant questioning about their outlaw relatives, the James boys (as the story goes). The names I have seen with Jesse are James M. White (born in TN.), and Joe (Joseph) White. (Not sure of the relationship to Mary) According to my info this is in the White line with John White born around 1822–26 TN and died 1874–80 in Wright Co. MO. His wife was Susan and his son was Daniel Pearce White b. 1857 TN.[223]

74. Wilkerson, Bill—A Jesse James connection. Bill Wilkerson rode with the James-Younger Gang and is "credited as a member at Clay County Savings Association Robbery, Liberty, Mo."[224]

I am convinced, due to strong supporting evidence, that the Bill Wilkerson who rode with the James-Younger Gang is the same one my great-great-grandfather referred to. His full name may have been William G. Wilkerson. This William G. Wilkerson in 1860 was a twenty-six-year-old white male who was born in Missouri and was still living there at that time in Platte Township, Clay County. Jesse and Frank James also lived in Clay County, Missouri, in 1860.

Census records indicate that there was a "William Wilkerson; Age 42; White male; Born in Missouri but living in Dallas, Texas in 1870." With the Missouri connection one wonders if there may have been a mistake with the age on the census record, and he may have been the Bill Wilkerson who rode with Jesse James. Census records also show that the Youngers also lived in Texas in 1870. "Difficulties in Missouri had caused them to head to Texas not long before this census. In January of the year following this census John got into serious trouble in Texas, indicted for the murder of a deputy sheriff. Jim Younger, himself, was a deputy sheriff in Dallas County 1870–71. Thomas is Cole Younger. John Harrison Younger, Cole Younger's brother, born 1851 in Missouri, was indicted for murder in Texas in January 1871 for killing a deputy sheriff who was attempting to arrest him. Killed by Pinkerton agents March 16, 1874."

Ted Yeatman of Tennessee, author of *Frank And Jesse James, The Story Behind The Legend*, vehemently denies that my great-great-grandfather may have been Jesse James. He said in his book, "[Betty] Duke's book makes reference to James and Bill Wilkerson, associated with Courtney, as 'known' members of the James-Younger Gang. In all of my years of research I have never encountered these names in connection with the gang."

In his rush to discredit my mother, Mr. Yeatman shot himself in the foot, as they say. He dedicated his book to Dr. William Settle, Jr., author of *Jesse James Was His Name*. Mr. Yeatman probably just overlooked the fact that Dr. Settle clearly states in his book that Bill Wilkerson was accused of taking part in the James-Younger Gang's robbery of the Clay County Savings Bank in Liberty, Missouri, on February 13, 1866. James Wilkerson was also a suspect and had ridden with Quantrill. Many other sources also wrote that both Bill and James Wilkerson rode with Jesse James. To cite two:

1. The Kansas City *Daily Journal of Commerce* wrote: "February 13, 1866, Liberty, Missouri: When James Love published the bank's offer of a $5,000 reward, he blamed the robbery on a band of bushwhackers, who reside chiefly in Clay County, and have their rendezvous on or near the Missouri River, above Sibley in Jackson County. At least nine men were named in succeeding days by witnesses to the robbery and pursuit: Ol' Shepard, Bud and Donnie Pence, *Jim and Bill Wilkerson* [italics added for emphasis], Frank Gregg, Joab Perry, and Redman Munkers."

[Although Munkers soon provided an alibi, supported by five witnesses.]

2. The *Liberty Tribune* (of Missouri) wrote: "James Wilkerson rode with Quantrell (Also spelled Quantrill); was credited as a member at Clay County Savings Association robbery, Liberty, Mo.; and was taken to St. Joseph, Mo. to identify Jesse's (Jesse James) body."

A Jessie Wilkerson is buried in Blevins Cemetery, in Blevins, Texas, who was born March 13, 1896, and died on December 1, 1973. Was this Bill Wilkerson's relative? With so much evidence pointing to the fact that my great-great-grandfather was Jesse James the odds are that the Bill Wilkerson he mentioned in his diary was the one who rode with Jesse James. Bill Wilkerson was obviously close to my great-great-grandfather or he wouldn't have been sitting with the family at Thomas Hudson Barron's death bed in 1874.

✹

My great-great-grandfather may have lived and died in Texas under a name other than his own, but he was surrounded by family and friends in Texas who didn't care what name he lived by.

NOTES

Many of my sources are from my late mother's research. Because the internet is constantly evolving, many of the websites she accessed are no longer available. I have noted this where applicable.

CHAPTER 1.
JESSE JAMES: THE TRADITIONAL STORY

1. Quoted in Donald Hale, *Quarterly of the National Association for Outlaw and Lawman History* 24, no. 2 (April–June 2000).
2. Frank Triplett, *Life and Tragic Death of Jesse James* (Penn.: E. E. Barley Co., 1883).
3. Joseph Rickards (Sheriff of Clay County, Missouri), "$5,000 Reward," Wanted poster, 1866–68. Reprinted by Jesse James Publishers, Liberty, Missouri.
4. *The Daily Gazette,* April 5, 1882. Zee Mimms' testimony at the coroner's inquest.
5. Bob, reply to "Jesse James My Father," by Betty Dorsett Duke, James Family Forum, Genealogy.com, Feb. 19, 2004.
6. Jack Wymore, ed., *Good Bye Jesse James: Six Major News Stories Concerning the Life, Death, and Funeral of America's Greatest Outlaw* (Liberty, Mo.: Jesse James Bank Museum, 1967), 116. First reported in 1882 in the *Kansas City Daily Journal.*
7. Wymore, *Good Bye Jesse James.*

8. Hale, *Quarterly of the National Association for Outlaw and Lawman History.*

9. D. H. Rule, "James and Youngers: The Life and Trial of Frank James," Civil War St. Louis website, accessed October 28, 2019.

10. John Newman Edwards, *Noted Guerrillas, or The Warfare on the Border* (St. Louis, Mo.: Bryan Brand, 1877), 167.

11. *St. Joseph Daily Gazette,* St. Joseph, Missouri, April 12, 1882. We have been unable to track down the author and title of the article, but believe this story may have also been reprinted as "Jesse's Ruse" in the *Savannah Democrat,* April 14, 1882.

12. Wilrena Calvert Miller, "The Courtney's [*sic*] of Clay County," *Pioneer Times* 10, no. 1, (Jan. 1986).

13. Miller, "The Courtney's [*sic*] of Clay County."

14. Posted by User ID *****9962, "Some Interesting New Info on the Courtney Issue," James Family Genealogy Forum, Genealogy.com, October 3, 2008.

15. "Marriage records of Clay County, Missouri, 1852–1900, vol. 2." The marriage date is given as Sept. 5, 1872. The marriage is listed as between James Courtney and Bettie Cole and was officiated by Asa Bird. Rootsweb.com.

16. "Marriage records of Clay County, Missouri 1852–1900, vol. 1–3," accessed September 22, 2021. The marriage date is given as March 30, 1865. The marriage is listed as between John M. Meret and Ann J. Courtney and was officiated by I. Montgomery. Rootsweb.com.

17. "Alexander Doniphan Pence," accessed December 16, 2019, Rootsweb .com.

18. "America Lurania Pence," accessed December 16, 2019, Rootsweb.com.

19. Miller, "The Courtney's [*sic*] of Clay County."

20. Posted by Bobby Jones, "James Family Forum: Frank & Home Guard," Genealogy.com, December 10, 2003.

21. Rose Mary Lankford, *The Encyclopedia of Quantrill's Guerrillas* (Evening Shade, Ark.: R.M., 1999).

22. Wymore, *Good Bye Jesse James.*

23. Document courtesy of Carol Holmes.

24. 1860 federal census record, Missouri, Johnson Co., Post Oak TWP, Series: M633 Roll: 626 Page: 965.

25. Miller, "The Courtney's [*sic*] of Clay County."

26. Jack Loftin, *Tales through Archer* (Burnet, Tex.: Eakin Publications, 1979).

CHAPTER 2.
BILLY THE KID: THE TRADITIONAL STORY

1. Wikipedia s.v. "Billy the Kid," accessed October 22, 2020.

2. W. C. Jameson, *Billy the Kid: Beyond the Grave* (Taylor Trade Publications, August 7, 2008), 10.

3. Jameson, *Billy the Kid,* 11.

4. Jameson, *Billy the Kid,* preface xii.

CHAPTER 3. IN CAHOOTS

1. Henry F. Hoyt, *A Frontier Doctor* (The Riverside Press, 1929), 110–11.

2. Bill Markley, *Billy the Kid and Jesse James: Outlaws of the Legendary West* (Rowman and Littlefield, September 27, 2019), 187.

3. Ted P. Yeatman, *Frank and Jesse James: The Story Behind the Legend* (Nashville: Cumberland House, 2000), 209.

4. Yeatman, *Frank and Jesse James,* 210.

5. Posted by Terry D. Smith, "The Limbs and Branches of the Smith Family Tree," Rootsweb.com, accessed September 22, 2021.

6. Brian Haines, "More to the Story: Missing Gold, DNA and the Old West," Hutchinsonleader.com, April 21, 2019.

CHAPTER 4.
OUTLAWS WITH A HIGHER PURPOSE

1. Duke, Betty Dorsett, *The Truth About Jesse James* (Greenwood Village, Colo.: Fiddler's Green Press, 2007), 448.

2. Interview with Don Jackson, Pecos County, Texas, 2009.

3. The Grand Lodge of Louisiana, "Grand Lodge of the Month for February 2020," February 1, 2020.

4. Randolph B. "Mike" Campbell, s.v. "Knights of the Golden Circle,"

Texas State Historical Association Handbook of Texas online, accessed July 15, 2020.

5. Dirk Johnson, "Following 1937 Story of Buried Gold, Family Searches New Mexico's Sands," *New York Times,* July 29, 1992.

6. Eric Veillette, "Billy the Kid, Boarder at Belle Starr's," Historiquement Logique website (in French), February 2014.

CHAPTER 5.
NEW FACES IN AN OLD PHOTOGRAPH

1. *Fort Worth Daily Gazette*, Vol. 13, no. 219, ed. 1 (Thursday, February 7, 1889). Accessed October 11, 2021 from the University of North Texas Libraries.

2. W. Leon Smith, *The Clifton Record*, Vol. 106, no. 34, ed. 1 (Friday, April 27, 2001). Accessed October 12, 2021 from the University of North Texas Libraries.

3. Smith, *The Clifton Record.*

4. Cecilia Rasmussen, "Truth Dims the Legend of Outlaw Queen Belle Starr." *Los Angeles Times.* (February 17, 2002).

5. Rasmussen, "Truth Dims the Legend of Outlaw Queen Belle Starr."

6. Bill Black, "Bell Starr: A Black Widow?" on the Fort Smith National Historic Site page of the National Park Service website, March 1996.

7. Leon C. Metz. "Starr, Myra Maybelle Shirley." *Handbook of Texas Online*, accessed October 12, 2021.

8. Wikipedia s.v. "Belle Starr," accessed October 12, 2021.

9. Wikipedia s.v. "Belle Starr," accessed October 12, 2021

10. History.com. "Belle Starr Murdered in Oklahoma," accessed October 12, 2021; A&E Television Networks, "This Day in History," February 2, 2021.

11. Encyclopedia.com, "Starr, Belle (1848–1889)," accessed October 12, 2021.

CHAPTER 6. FAMILY TIES

1. Citation from the Individual Family Records Family Data Collection of Ancestry.com shows that John James and Dinah Allen did marry in 1735

in Virginia. "Name: John James; Spouse: Dinah Allen; Parents: Thomas James and Sarah Mason: Birth Place: Stafford CO, VA., Birth Date: 16 Mar 1707; Marriage Place: Stafford CO, VA; Marriage Date: Before 6 Aug 1738; Death Place: Fauquier CO, Hamilton Parish, VA Death Date: 25 May 1778."

2. Edmund West, compiler. Individual Family Records Family Data Collection of Ancestry.com. 1810 federal census record for Goochland, VA, and 1820 census record for Russellville, KY, courtesy of Laura Way.

3. Barbee's Crossroads website, "Andrew Barbee Line," site no longer accessible.

4. Carol Holmes, reply to Banditoutlaw13, "Your Barbee family lived in Liberty, Clay County Missouri," August 24, 2007.

5. What follows was provided to us courtesy of genealogist Laura Way. "John Jordan Crittenden: Born near Versailles, Woodford County, Ky., September 10, 1786. Illinois territory attorney general, 1809-10; member of Kentucky state house of representatives, 1811-17, 1825-29; served in the U.S. Army during the War of 1812; U.S. Senator from Kentucky, 1817-19, 1835-41, 1842-48, 1855-61; Presidential Elector for Kentucky, 1824; U.S. District Attorney for Kentucky, 1827-29; U.S. Attorney General, 1841, 1850-53; Governor of Kentucky, 1848-50; U.S. Representative from Kentucky 8th District, 1861-63. Two of his sons were generals on opposite sides in the Civil War; a grandson of his was killed in Gen. Custer's expedition against the Sioux in 1876. Died in Frankfort, Franklin County, Ky., July 26, 1863. Interment at Frankfort Cemetery, Frankfort, Ky. Crittenden County, Ky. is named for him." George Norbury Mackenzie, *Filson Club History Quarterly* 51 (April 1977): 125-42. "Colonial Families of the United States," Volume VI. (Baltimore: Genealogical Publishing Co. Inc., 1907), 189.

6. "Grafteron Thomason," Ancestry.com: "Grafteron Thomason b 1816 Scott Co. KY d 1882 Platte Co. MO Classification: Obituary Surnames: Thomason, Talbott, Everett, Hale, Timberlake Liberty Weekly Tribune Missouri 1 Mar 3 1882."

7. Philip W. Steele, *Jesse and Frank James: The Family History* (Gretna, Louisiana, Pelican Publishing, July 1987).

8. Interview with Ray Holt on Rootsweb.com.

9. Email from Carol Holmes to Betty Dorsett Duke dated Nov. 4, 2007.

CHAPTER 7.
WITH FAITH COMES POWER

1. Roger Finke and Rodney Stark, *The Churching of America, 1776–2005: Winners and Losers in Our Religious Economy.* (United Kingdom: Rutgers University Press, 2005), abstract available online.

2. Nathan O. Hatch, "The Puzzle of American Methodism," *Church History*, 63 (1994): 183.

3. Hatch, "The Puzzle of American Methodism," 179.

4. Roger Finke and Rodney Stark, "How the Upstart Sects Won America 1776–1850," *Journal for the Scientific Study of Religion,* 28:1 (March 1989): 42.

5. J. H. Spencer, "A History of Kentucky Baptists," Baptist History Homepage website. Written in 1885, accessed July 7, 2020.

6. Rev. Joseph Bledsoe, "Jane Baylor (Bledsoe)," geni.com, accessed September 22, 2021.

7. Travis L. Summerlin, s.v. "Baylor, Robert Emmett Bledsoe 1793–1873," Texas State Historical Association Handbook of Texas online, accessed July 10, 2020.

8. Wikipedia, s.v. "Thomas Chilton," accessed September 22, 2021.

9. Thomas W. Cutrer, s.v. "Chilton, George William (1828–1883)," Texas State Historical Association Handbook of Texas online, accessed July 14, 2020.

10. Randolph B. "Mike" Campbell, s.v. "Knights of the Golden Circle," Texas State Historical Association Handbook of Texas online, accessed July 15, 2020.

11. Wikipedia, s.v. "George W. L. Bickley," accessed July 20, 2020.

12. Mark Twain, *Life On the Mississippi* (Boston: James R. Osgood, 1883), 557.

13. "Henry Clay Dean," *St. Louis Post-Dispatch,* St. Louis, Missouri, December 1, 1882, p 4.

14. Gerard S. Patrone, *Judgement at Gallatin: The Trial of Frank James* (Lubbock: Texas Tech University Press, 1998), 82.

15. Edward E. Leslie, *The Devil Knows How to Ride: The True Story of William Clarke Quantrill and his Confederate Raiders* (Boston: Da Capo Press, 1996), 192.

CHAPTER 8. BURIED TREASURE

1. United Press International Archives, "A New James Gang Digs for Jesse James Safe," upi.com, August 16, 1992.

CHAPTER 9. MODERN REACH
OF AN OLD WEST OUTLAW

1. Betty Dorsett Duke, *Jesse James: The Smoking Gun* (Liberty Hill, Tex: Fiddler's Green, 2011), 161.
2. Ferd Kaufman, "Billie Sol Estes, Texas Con Man Whose Fall Shook Up Washington, Dies at 88," *New York Times,* May 14, 2013.
3. Ferd Kaufman "Billie Sol Estes."
4. Ferd Kaufman "Billie Sol Estes."

CHAPTER 10. FURTHERING
THE LIGHT OF FREEDOM AND LIBERTY

1. Pope Leo XIII, *The Pope and the Freemasons: The Letter "Humanum Genus" of the Pope, Leo XIII, against Free-Masonry and the Spirit of the Age* (Westphalia Press: Washington D.C., 2013), 2.
2. Adam Willis, "Ahoy, Mateys! Thar Be Jewish Pirates!" Jewish Journal online, September 15, 2006.

APPENDIX.
CONNECTIONS THAT PAVED THE WAY

1. Joanne C. Eakin and Donald R. Hales, *Branded as Rebels: A List of Bushwhackers, Guerrillas, Partisan Rangers, Confederates and Southern Sympathizers from Missouri during the War Years* (1993).
2. James, Thurston, *James-Younger Gang Journal,* Summer 2003 issue, page 5.
3. *St. Louis Daily Missouri Republican,* May 1, 1872; *The Kentucky Explorer,* November 1988.
4. Posted by Barbara Hathaway, "My Families; Entries: 32311," June 4, 2004," Ancestry.com.
5. Posted by Barbara Hathaway, "My Families; Entries: 32311."

6. Marilyn Chandler provided information to this author; see also Joanne Chiles Eakin, *Missouri Prisoners of War From Gratiot Street Prison & Myrtle Street Prison, St. Louis, MO and Alton Prison, Alton, Illinois Including Citizens, Confederates, Bushwhackers and Guerrillas* (Independence, Mo.: J. C. Eakin, 1995).

7. Eakin, *Missouri Prisoners of War.*

8. Posted by Will and Karla Beauchamp, "E.L. ANDRUSS / YAVALET ANDRUSS," Ancestry.com Message Board, November 17, 2000.

9. Jonathan K. T. Smith, "My Riverside Cemetery Tombstone Inscriptions Scrapbook," Records & Data, TNGenWeb.org from pages 35–38: "Whig and Tribune, Jackson, Aug. 24, 1872: Death of Rev./Col W. M. Dunavay (*sic*), mayor-elect of Jackson, Aug. 22, in home of son-in-law, James V. Anderson, Jackson. Grand Master, Grand Lodge of Tenn. (Masons)."

10. Texas State Library and Archives Commission Confederate Indigent Families Index: "Claimant Name: Andruss, Margaret E; Application Number: 33999; County: Montague; Husband: Andruss, Harvey Adolphus."

11. Eakin and Hale, *Branded as Rebels*

12. Eakin and Hale, *Branded as Rebels.*

13. Mae Courtney Thompson, "Jim Courtney, Texan." She wrote, "You may wonder why he would not stop there (Nebraska) but it seems that he had connections in Texas and a commitment to come to a certain place."

14. Mae Courtney, personal communication.

15. Falls County Historical Commission, *Families of Falls County, Texas* (Austin: Eakin Press, 1987).

16. Texas Genealogy and Texas History Notes: Some of the information of this writing is from pages of a Falls County Publication sent to me by a descendant of J. G. W.'s third marriage. Author unknown. Military Record: A Mounted Gunman, San Augine Volunteers, 3rd Brigade of Republic of Texas Militia (1836-1845) apt. of Company of Washington County Volunteers, "Regiment of Rangers" east side of the Brazos River (Jun 30, 1836-Jul 19, 1836).

17. Barron Family Forum: "Betty Hunn Buckley," Genealogy.com, May 9, 2000, post #1142.

18. Waco Tribune Herald, July 2, 1976. Reproduced by Moody Texas Ranger Memorial Library, Waco, Texas.

19. Posted by John C. Barron (ID *****3661) "Barron Family Genealogy Forum: Re: Milam & Travis Barron," Genealogy.com, March 1, 2004.

20. "Falls County Bios Board," Falls County, TXGenWeb project.

21. Charles Rush, "Civil War Veterans of Falls County," Falls County TxGenWeb project; "Falls County Cemetery List of Civil War Veterans," Falls County TexGenWeb project.

22. Typed by Theresa Carhart, "Blackwell, W. J., July 12, 1907," Falls County TXGenWeb project.

23. Posted by Becky, "Blackwell Family Genealogy Forum, J. Blackwell, Pike Co., AR," Genealogy.com, February 2, 2000, post #1133.

24. G. Zeman, ed., Vicksburg National Military Park Home Page, "Troops in the Defense of Vicksburg—Confederate; 5th Missouri Cavalry."

25. Ancestry.com Civil War Records.

26. Posted by Jeanette Theilacker, "Blackwell Family Forum," Genealogy .com, November 12, 1998.

27. "1870 federal census record for Waco, McLennan County, Texas," Ancestry.com.

28. Information supplied by Jimmy and Helen Thornton, "The Grand Lodge of Texas 1873 Proceeding Annual Communication," Carolina Lodge, Number 330, District 17.

29. Heritage Quest online census records.

30. Rush, "Civil War Veterans of Falls County," Falls County TxGenWeb project.

31. Posted by Donna Shreeve in reply to Bob, "Z.D. Bonner, Blacksmith," Genealogy.com, February 4, 2002, post #1272.

32. Steve Wilson, Oklahoma Treasures and Treasure Tales (Norman, University of Oklahoma Press, 1976).

33. Posted by Sarah Glover in reply to Roxie Riley, "Christopher Columbus Bonner," Bonner Family Forum, Genealogy.com, May 10, 2001, Post #1045.

34. Rush, "Civil War Veterans of Falls County," Falls County TxGenWeb project.

35. Eakin and Hale, Branded as Rebels.

36. Heritage Quest online census records.

37. "Brushy Bill—The Truth?" from a frontpage website no longer accessible.

38. "Billy the Kid and Jesse James," from an angelfire website no longer accessible.

39. Bob Brewer, personal email to this author, June 4, 2004. Brewer coauthored *Shadow of the Sentinel* with Warren Getler (New York: Simon & Schuster, 2003).

40. Heritage Quest online census records.

41. Posted by Nancy E. Broomfield in reply to Jean Masoner, "Broomfields in Missouri and Kentucky," Broomfield Family Forum, Genealogy.com, October 2, 2000.

42. Frank Triplett, *The Life and Tragic Death of Jesse James* (Penn.: E. E. Barclay Co., 1883, reprinted by Triton).

43. Eakin and Hale, *Branded as Rebels*.

44. Eakin and Hale, *Branded as Rebels*.

45. "Civil War Service Records: Woodson S. Broomfield," Ancestry.com.

46. Posted by Nancy E. Broomfield in reply to Jean Masoner, "Broomfields in Missouri and Kentucky."

47. Lankford, *The Encyclopedia of Quantrill's Guerrillas*.

48. In personal communication, Doris Spidel reported that she was also Frank Krause's relative and lived with him. She told my mother they lived next to my great-great-grandfather.

49. Heritage Quest online census record.

50. 1850 Bates Co., MO, Being, ED: 6, page 539, HH 601, Ancestry.com image 81 of 84.

51. Charles W. "Bill" Henderson, personal communication.

52. 1870 Denton Co., TX Census, Elizabethtown P. O., Pct. 4, page 26, HH 183–199, Ancestry.com image 178 of 192.

53. "Burnett Family and Other Branches Entries: 53582," Rootsweb.com, updated October 16, 2007.

54. "BURNETT-US-L Archives: June Bork: [BURNETT-US] Burnett/Johnson/Younger connections," Rootsweb.com.

55. "Federal census record - Series: T624, Roll: 1550, Part: 2, Page: 25A, Year: 1910," Ancestry.com.

56. Information courtesy of Juanita Martin.

57. Information courtesy of Juanita Martin.

58. Posted by Brownie MacKie in reply to Charles C., "Cage family of

Madison Co. MS," Cage Family Forum, Genealogy.com, April 4, 2000, post #65.

59. Posted by Brownie MacKie in reply to Milton Cage, "Milton Cage," Cage Family Forum, Genealogy.com. Will: Halifax county VA Will Book 12, Pg. 93 Sept. 16, 1820.

60. "Rosalie's Family" on a bravepages website no longer accessible.

61. "Texas Census, 1820–90; Cage JAMES; State: Texas; Year: 1860; County: Erath County Record Type: Slave schedule; Township: Beat 1, Page: 290," Ancestry.com; Voter Registration: 8-17-67; James H. Cage; Pct. 1; In State: 9 years; In Pct.: 9 years; Native: Texas.

62. Information courtesy of Juanita Martin.

63. 1870 federal census records, Ancestry.com.

64. Eakin and Hale, *Branded as Rebels*.

65. Gloria B. Mayfield and Veda Bragg Mendoza, "Blevins Cemetery, Falls County," Cemeteries of Texas website, submitted by Theresa Carhart.

66. Mayfield and Mendoza, "Blevins Cemetery, Falls County."

67. 1870 federal census, Ancestry.com.

68. Lankford, *Encyclopedia of Quantrill's Guerrillas*.

69. Posted by crolholmes, "Members of Quantrill's Guerrillas in the Civil War," James Family Forum, Genealogy.com, May 28, 2002, message 14562 of 35971.

70. Lankford, *Encyclopedia of Quantrill's Guerrillas*.

71. 1870 census record, Ancestry.com; the post also references Journal of Missouri's 24th General Assembly, KCG, Vol.22, #1.

72. Heritage Quest online.

73. Sue Duncan, "Franklin & Murdock Entries: 4337," Rootsweb.com.

74. Posted by Jane Webb in reply to Shirley Starks, "Cates in Wise Co, TX (1860)," Cates Family Genealogy Forum, March 6, 2004, Genealogy .com.

75. "Robert Cates," Cates Family Forum, Genealogy.com.

76. "Civil War Service Records," Ancestry.com.

77. Texas 1870 Federal Census Index 1820–1890; Federal Population Schedule.

78. Courtesy of the Wise County Sheriff's Department, 2003.

79. Posted by Tricia Cates, Ancestry.com.

80. Edward E. Leslie, *The Devil Knows How to Ride: The True Story of William Clarke Quantrill and His Confederate Raiders* (Boston, De Capo Press, 1998), 100.

81. Posted by Linda Snyder, "Dalton Family Forum," Genealogy.com.

82. Rush, "Civil War Veterans of Falls County," TxGenWeb project.

83. Posted by Jimmie Lois Ezell Dixon in reply to Betty, "Clarks and The James Gang," Clarks Family Forum, Genealogy.com, July 8, 2004.

84. Eakin and Hale, *Branded as Rebels*.

85. Carol Holmes, "Subject: Letter from Frank James on Jim Cummings," December 30, 2004.

86. Heritage Quest online census records.

87. Julia Whatley, "An Historical Account of the Blevins Cemetery Falls County, Texas 1875–1993."

88. Submitted by Ken Gates, "John Clark," TXGenWeb project.

89. Submitted by Ken Gates, "Falls County Bios Taken from Families of Falls County," TXGenWeb project.

90. "Falls County Bios; James Lafayette Courtney Biography," TXGenWeb project.

91. Lankford, *Encyclopedia of Quantrill's Guerrillas*.

92. Falls County Historical Commission, *Families of Falls County*.

93. Clifton Pepper, "Pepper-Lomax Entries: 21517," Rootsweb.com, updated June 20, 2006.

94. Information supplied by Jimmy & Helen Thornton, "The Grand Lodge of Texas 1873 Proceeding Annual Communication."

95. Linda Snyder in reply to crolholmes, "Re: Jesse Cole, suicide?" James Family Forum, Genealogy.com, July 29, 2003.

96. Wilson, *Oklahoma Treasures and Treasure Tales*.

97. "The James-Younger Gang Homepage, The Other Guys," on an islandnet .com website no longer accessible.

98. Heritage Quest online census records.

99. 1870 federal census record, Ancestry.com.

100. "Bios: A. Harry Williams; Selected and converted. American Memory, Library of Congress. Washington, 1994." Rootsweb.com.

101. World War I Draft Registration cards (Part IV) from DeSoto Parish, Louisiana listed under "Black Men from towns other than Logansport," Rootsweb.com.

102. Submitted by Grant W. Johnston, "Wallace Cemetery, DeSoto Parish, Louisiana," Rootsweb.com. Johnston lists his source as Amos Barron, *Cemetery Book,* 1967.

103. Douglas Henry, "Entry 316573," Rootsweb; 1860 Denton County, Missouri Census, Spears Mill, Page 94, HH 660–661, Ancestry.com image 94 of 125.

104. Posted by Patricia Thompson in reply to Betty Dorsett Duke, "James Prince Cates," Cates Family Forum, Genealogy.com, November 6, 2006.

105. "Genealogy Records Collection of Robert Powell Carver," Rootsweb. com, page published on November 20, 1998 by Nancy P. Goodman.

106. Posted by David Crudup in reply to John L. Patterson, "Rebecca Temple Crudup, bn. 18 Oct. 1856," Crudup Family Forum, Genealogy.com, November 24, 1998, post #11.

107. Posted by John L. Patterson in reply to David Crudup, "Rebecca Temple Crudup, bn. 18 Oct. 1856," Crudup Family Forum, Genealogy.com, December 10, 1998, post #13.

108. Posted by John L. Patterson in reply to David Crudup, "Rebecca Temple Crudup, bn. 18 Oct. 1856," Post #13.

109. "Falls County Bios Board," TXGenWeb project.

110. Posted by Walt Nichols, "Alonzo Davis - KS/CO 1880s-1920s," Davis Family Forum, Genealogy.com, April 28, 2000.

111. Posted by Walt Nichols, "Alonzo Davis - KS/CO 1880s-1920s," Davis Family Forum, Genealogy.com, April 30, 2000.

112. Genealogical information provided courtesy of Carol Holmes.

113. Heritage quest online census records.

114. Posted by Beverly Shackelford, Devers Family Forum, Genealogy.com, January 19, 2001.

115. Lankford, *Encyclopedia of Quantrill's Guerrillas.*

116. Eakin and Hale, *Branded as Rebels.*

117. Posted by Susan Westerlaken, "Westerlaken Entries: 2252," Rootsweb. com, October 8, 2005.

118. 1870 United States Federal Census, Ancestry.com.

119. Heritage Quest online census records.

120. Private email from Michael Thomas Ellison, June 5, 2005.

121. Rush, "Civil War Veterans of Falls County," Falls County TxGenWeb project.

122. Rush, "Civil War Veterans of Falls County," Falls County TxGenWeb project. Ref. Castel.

123. Posted by Kit Cockrum in reply to Bubba Heitman, "J.C. Ervin," Ervin Family Forum, Genealogy.com, August 3, 2004.

124. Posted by Greg Smith, "Gregory Alan and Patrice Diane (Moore) Smith Family File Entries: 144928," Rootsweb.com, August 12, 2006.

125. Posted by Greg Smith, "Gregory Alan and Patrice Diane (Moore) Smith Family File Entries: 144928," Rootsweb.com, August 12, 2006. Contact: Greg Smith.

126. Heritage Quest online census records.

127. Posted by Glynda, "Blame it on Farley!" James Family Genealogy Forum, Genealogy.com, January 21, 2004.

128. Posted by Chas Alcock, "Southwest Louisiana Entries: 127519," Rootsweb.com, updated August 8, 2004.

129. Courtesy of the Wilbur Zink Collection.

130. Heritage Quest online census records.

131. Information courtesy of Carol Holmes. "Carol Watson" to "Jimmy Kerr" Subject: Gallaways, Rootsweb.com, June 3, 2001.

132. Posted by mv, "Quantrill's First Raid, the So-Called 'Freedom Raid,'" James Family Forum, Genealogy.com, January 12, 2003.

133. Posted by mv, "Quantrill's First Raid, the So-Called 'Freedom Raid,'" January 12, 2003.

134. Grayson County Frontier Village, *History of Grayson County, Texas,* 2 vols. (Winston-Salem, N.C.: Hunter, 1979, 1981).

135. Eakin and Hale, *Branded as Rebels.*

136. Rush, "Civil War Veterans of Falls County," Falls County TxGenWeb project.

137. Posted by Sherry Ohern, "Sherry Givens Ohern Entries: 2161," Rootsweb. com.

138. Posted by R. Leonard, "James D. Harding-a/ka/ Witter Hardin/Harden," Hardin Family Forum, Genealogy.com, February 4, 2002.

139. "1860," Ancestry.com.

140. "History of the James-Younger Gang: The Members of The James-Younger Gang," from an angelfire website no longer accessible.

141. Eakin and Hale, *Branded as Rebels.* The source cites Edwards, CSRJC.

142. Kathy Reynard, "The Courtney/Haun Family" on Jesse James In Texas? website, hosted by ericjames.org.

143. Jesse James a.k.a. James L. Courtney's personal diaries, 1871–1876.

144. Posted by Barbara Hathaway, "Entries: 36796," Rootsweb.com.

145. Lankford, *Encyclopedia of Quantrill's Guerrillas.*

146. Eakin and Hale, *Branded as Rebels.* The source cites Hale.

147. Lankford, *Encyclopedia of Quantrill's Guerrillas.*

148. Phillip Steele, *Jesse and Frank James: The Family History* (Gretna: Pelican Publishing, 1994).

149. Posted by Terry D. Smith, "The Limbs and Branches of the Smith Family Tree Entries: 270376," Rootsweb.com.

150. "Descendants of Edward Eidson Sr.-5-23/101Fourth Generation," from an imt.net site no longer available.

151. Dorothy Sloan Books, Ranching Catalogue Part 1; "John Chisum: Cattle Baron, Trail Blazer," from a homestead.com site no longer accessible.

152. "Nathan Bedford Forrest (1821–1877)" CivilWarHome.com.

153. "Eidson Family," from an imt.net site no longer available.

154. "The Kansas Cowboy—John Nathan Hittson," from droversmercantile. com, no longer accessible.

155. Charles Kenner, Handbook of Texas Online s.v. "John Hittson," accessed December 3, 2021.

156. Michael Trevis, "Palo Pinto Country Historical Markers: Hittson Cemetary," Fort Tours website, accessed December 3, 2021.

157. Posted by Bryan Hunt, "Hunts That Rode with the James Gang," Hunt Family Forum, Genealogy.com, July 05, 1999.

158. Posted by Bryan Hunt, "Hunts That Rode with the James Gang."

159. Heritage Quest online census records.

160. Carl Breihan, *Quantrill and His Guerrillas* (Denver: Sage Books, Denver, 1959).

161. Eakin and Hale, *Branded as Rebels.*

162. Heritage Quest online census records.

163. Lankford, *Encyclopedia of Quantrill's Guerrillas.*

164. TXGenWeb. "Falls County Military History."

165. Gloria B. Mayfield and Veda Bragg Mendoza, "Blevins Cemetery, Falls County."

166. Posted by Don Jackson in reply to Charles Cash, "Jackson's of Falls Co.,

TX," Jackson Family Forum, Genealogy.com, December 31, 2004, post #17539.

167. Posted by Don Jackson in reply to Charles Cash, "Jackson's of Falls Co, TX."

168. Lankford, *Encyclopedia of Quantrill's Guerrillas.*

169. Posted by Tracy Collier Hart in reply to Steve Mashburn, reply to "Bob(?) Jordan of the Jordan Gang," Genealogy.com, February 12, 2005, post #8596.

170. Posted by Connie Ward, "Bob(?) Jordan of the Jordan Gang," Jordan Family Forum, Genealogy.com, March 8, 1999.

171. Posted by Charlotte Sasek in reply to Jerry Leon Jordan, "Bob(?) Jordan of the Jordan Gang," Jordan Family Forum, Genealogy.com, March 11, 1999, post #1026.

172. Posted by Veronica Lynn Jordan in reply to Charlotte Sasek, "Bob(?) Jordan of the Jordan Gang," Jordan Family Forum, Genealogy.com, November 3, 2000, post #4257.

173. Eakin and Hale, *Branded as Rebels.*

174. Posted by prpletr Beeston. "Good-Engle-Hanks Entries." Rootsweb.com.

175. Mack White, "The Secret Life of Jesse James," Bison Bill's Weird West website.

176. Posted by TR Darr, "Darr Family Tree," Rootsweb.com.

177. Posted by Mary L. Katschke, "Genealogy Research Records of Mary (Jennings) Katschke," Rootsweb.com. The source cites Barron, John C. Letter to M. L. Katschke dated September 15, 1989.

178. "The James-Younger Gang Home Page" from an islandnet.com site no longer available.

179. Floyd D. P. Oydegaard, "Chronology of Jesse James," specific page no longer available.

180. Marley Brant, *Outlaws: The Illustrated History Of The James-Younger Gang* (Montgomery, Alabama: Elliott & Clark Publishing, 1997).

181. Eakin and Hale, *Branded as Rebels.*

182. Eakin and Hale, *Branded as Rebels.*

183. Posted by Gay Mathis, "Notorious Thompson McDaniels—Bank Robber—1875—Newspaper Article," U.S. Outlaws Forum, Genealogy .com, February 9, 2005.

184. Mayfield and Mendoza, "Blevins Cemetery, Falls County," Cemeteries of Texas website, submitted by Theresa Carhart.

185. Personal email from Ruth to this author, September 3, 2004.

186. Lankford, *Encyclopedia of Quantrill's Guerrillas.*

187. United States Federal Census, Clay Co., Missouri, 1830–70, Ancestry.com.

188. Theresa Carhart, "Falls County Bios," TxGenWeb Project.

189. Lankford, *Encyclopedia of Quantrill's Guerrillas.*

190. Lankford, *Encyclopedia of Quantrill's Guerrillas.*

191. Missouri Census, 1830–1870, Ancestry.com.

192. Heritage Quest online census records.

193. Eakin and Hale, *Branded as Rebels.*

194. David Minor, Handbook of Texas Online s.v. "Red River County, TX—Biographies—George B. Pickett," accessed December 8, 2021.

195. Posted by Elaine Poag Boushka, "File Entries: 17517," Rootsweb.com, May 19, 2005.

196. "Greer Frontier, The Empire of Greer County, Texas." *Magnum Daily Star*, (July 21, 1935, Sec A Page 1-4).

197. No author, Handbook of Texas Online s.v. "Day Land and Cattle Company," accessed December 8, 2021.

198. Posted by Shelba Davis in reply to David Hedgpeth, "Reed connection in TX to Jesse James?" Reed Family Forum, Genealogy.com, January 3, 2000.

199. Eakin and Hale, *Branded as Rebels.*

200. Rush, "Civil War Veterans of Falls County," Falls County TxGenWeb project.

201. Heritage Quest online census records.

202. Edward E. Leslie, "Quantrill's Bones," *American Heritage* magazine online 46 no. 4 (July/August 1995).

203. "The James-Younger Gang Homepage, The Other Guys," on an islandnet .com website no longer accessible.

204. T. J. Stiles, *Jesse James: Last Rebel of the Civil War* (New York: Vintage Books, 2002).

205. Stiles, *Jesse James.*

206. Online census records.

207. Eakin and Hale, *Branded as Rebels.*

208. Rush, "Civil War Veterans of Falls County," Falls County TxGenWeb project.

209. Census records from Lamar County, Texas, pg 143 Prec 6 1860, shows the Densman family in Texas.

210. *St. Joseph News Herald,* July 9, 1863.

211. Eakin and Hale, *Branded as Rebels.*

212. Heritage Quest online census records.

213. Jim Jennings, "Waggoner Ranch," *The Quarter Horse Journal,* posted on the AQHA website.

214. David Minor, Handbook of Texas Online s.v. "Alison, Texas."

215. "Reminiscenses of T. J. Waggoner, February 27, 1934," Rootsweb.com.

216. James McGuire interview by Lettie Major, manuscript/mixed material. Part of the U.S. Work Projects Administration, Federal Writers' Project. Available on the Library of Congress website.

217. H. Allen Anderon, Handbook of Texas Online s.v. "Waggoner Ranch."

218. Posted by Susan Hayden in reply to Ray Kenser, "Any Walker That Ran with Jesse James/Younger/Etc.?" Genealogy.com, November 17, 2002.

219. Posted by Mike Venable, "Complete List—Quantrills Raiders," Geneaology.com, April 22, 2004.

220. Edward E. Leslie, *The Devil Knows How to Ride: The True Story Of William Clarke Quantril And His Confederate Raiders* (New York: Hatchett Books, 1998), 77.

221. Carol Holmes to Betty Dorsett Duke. Information after the first paragraph comes from the Falls County Historical Commission, *Families of Falls County* (Austin: Eakin Press), 478.

222. Eakin and Hale, *Branded as Rebels.*

223. White Family Genealogy Forum

224. "The James-Younger Gang Homepage, The Other Guys," on an islandnet .com website no longer accessible.

Index

Page numbers in *italics* refer to illustrations.

BOOKS OF RELATED INTEREST

The Mysterious Life and Faked Death of Jesse James
Based on Family Records, Forensic Evidence, and His Personal Journals
by Daniel J. Duke and Teresa F. Duke

Jesse James and the Lost Templar Treasure
Secret Diaries, Coded Maps, and the Knights of the Golden Circle
by Daniel J. Duke

Templar Sanctuaries in North America
Sacred Bloodlines and Secret Treasures
by William F. Mann
Foreword by Scott F. Wolter

The Last Refuge of the Knights Templar
The Ultimate Secret of the Pike Letters
by William F. Mann

Rosicrucian America
How a Secret Society Influenced the Destiny of a Nation
by Steven Sora

The Lost Treasure of the Knights Templar
Solving the Oak Island Mystery
by Steven Sora

The Ancient Giants Who Ruled America
The Missing Skeletons and the Great Smithsonian Cover-Up
by Richard J. Dewhurst

First Templar Nation
How Eleven Knights Created a New Country and a Refuge for the Grail
by Freddy Silva

INNER TRADITIONS • BEAR & COMPANY
P.O. Box 388
Rochester, VT 05767
1-800-246-8648
www.InnerTraditions.com

Or contact your local bookseller